YOGA MYTHOLOGY

Devdutt Pattanaik, renowned mythologist from India, author of over 50 books and over 1000 columns on the subject, and a TED speaker, has written and illustrated this book. He has structured it in a way that makes the subject accessible to an international audience.

Matthew Rulli, former Marine and an experienced registered yoga teacher (E-RYT 500) from the USA, who has been studying Sanskrit and Eastern philosophy for over a decade, felt the need for such a book amongst yoga enthusiasts and initiated this project by contacting Devdutt Pattanaik in 2017. Over the next two years, he listed asanas and served as the model, photographer and commentator for the 64 postures finally selected for this book.

Also by Devdutt Pattanaik

Shiva to Shankara: Giving Form to the Formless

Culture: 50 Insights from Mythology

Leader: 50 Insights from Mythology

Faith: 40 Insights into Hindu Mythology

YOGA MYTHOLOGY

64 ASANAS AND THEIR STORIES

Devdutt Pattanaik
with Matthew Rulli

Illustrations by Devdutt Pattanaik
Photographs of, and by, Matthew Rulli

Harper
Collins

First published in hardback in India by
HarperCollins *Publishers* in 2019
A-75, Sector 57, Noida, Uttar Pradesh 201301, India
www.harpercollins.co.in

2 4 6 8 10 9 7 5 3 1

P-ISBN: 9789353570842
E-ISBN: 9789353570859

Typeset in Garamond by Special Effects Graphics Design Co., Mumbai

Printed and bound at
Thomson Press (India) Ltd

Contents

Vishnu

Dedication and Acknowledgements

To the many generations of students and teachers of yoga, especially those who have helped me experience yoga in this life: from the simplicity of The Yoga Institute (Yogendra school) to the precision of the Iyengar school.

Devdutt Pattanaik

I would like to dedicate my contribution to this book to my teachers: Dave, whose love of stories like these ignited my own fascination for yoga mythology, and Cheryl, whose friendship, guidance and wisdom have been some of the greatest influences on my life.

And to my son, Bradley, for teaching me that I could truly love and care for someone more than myself, and for being the sweetest, most compassionate person that I have ever known – I adore you.

My sincerest gratitude to Devdutt. When I first considered the idea of writing a book on yoga mythology, I knew that, even after years of research, I would never be able to produce a work worthy of the subject matter, especially after reading books like Devdutt's *Jaya*, *Indian Mythology* and the Seven Secrets series. When I sent him an email, I didn't even expect a response, and I certainly didn't expect an invitation to work together on the project. It has been a tremendous privilege and honour, not only to be involved in the making of the book, but also to share a creative space with such an inspiring and brilliant mind.

I would also like to thank my mother and the rest of my family for their boundless love and support. Leo, for the friendship and for introducing me to yoga in the first place. My teachers, Carlyn, Marivic, Julie and John, for their dedication to sharing their knowledge and preserving the yoga tradition. The gurus, Patanjali, Shri T. Krishnamacharya, Srivatsa Ramaswami, Pattabhi and Sharath Jois, B.K.S. Iyengar, and all those who helped to carry the gift of yoga through the ages.

And finally, my thanks to you, the reader, for without your interest and support, this book would not be possible. I hope it inspires in you as much fascination and appreciation for the indescribable depth and richness that this mythology gives to the practice of yoga as it has for me.

Matthew Rulli

Authors' Note

This is not a book on the practice of yoga.
This is about the mythology that nurtured the idea of yoga.

We live in times when the Buddha has become a spa icon, and the pursuit of health has been reduced to losing weight and developing a six-pack to indulge vanity. People see health as a secular activity, divorced from religion or spirituality, which are either disdainfully dismissed or expressed with unnecessary aggression. Few acknowledge the psychological and social role played by faith, or the relationship between the physical, the psychological and the social. It has become difficult to speak of yoga without plunging into acrimonious debates on whether it is simply a fitness regime or if there is anything spiritual (mystical or occult), religious (Hindu or Buddhist or Jain) or cultural (Indian) about it.

Radical Hindus, including those who do not live in India any more, tend to be territorial about yoga and insist on looking at it as puritanical (a colonial hangover) and devotional, ignoring the role of sensuous yoginis, and the importance of magical powers associated with yogis, in folklore. They fear yoga is being culturally appropriated by the West, in response to which many Western academicians have sought to strip yoga of its roots, arguing that modern yoga owes more to European colonizers and American entrepreneurship and less to Indian sages, or Hindu customs and beliefs.

To avoid controversy, therefore, and to ensure that the benefit of yoga reaches a wide audience, many yoga teachers dissociate yoga from its heritage and make it more about health than about wisdom; more about the body and less about the mind, and even less about the spirit. As a result, few who practice yoga around the world are aware of the underlying yoga philosophy, and even fewer are aware of yoga mythology: stories, symbols and rituals that shaped the worldview in which yoga was nurtured for over 3000 years. This book hopes to fill this knowledge gap in a manner and tone that is playful, rather than pedantic; it presents *a* truth, not *the* truth.

Many find the use of the word 'Indian' problematic, insisting instead on geographical phrases like South Asia or specific religious qualifications like Hindu or Buddhist or Jain. This is the malaise of academicians in the humanities who seek to compete with the precision of the pure sciences. This book uses the word 'Indic' loosely to refer to ideas that primarily originated and were nurtured in the Indian subcontinent (South Asia) and which, even today, dominate both cultural and religious expression in the region.

This is not a manual for asanas, though we have put forth some thoughts on the postures. The postures listed in this book may be given a different name by a different yoga school. We have included a few variations to demonstrate this. Indic culture shuns standardization. Every guru customizes their knowledge based on their own capacity and experience, and that of their students. Everything has hundreds of variations and improvisations, with a broad common theme aligning the seemingly misaligned. So please read *Yoga Mythology* keeping in mind that:

Within infinite myths lies an eternal truth
Who sees it all?
Varuna has but a thousand eyes
Indra, a hundred
You and I, only two

Introduction
Yoga's Narrative Canvas

Under the Pole Star, atop Mount Kailas, that mountain of stone covered with snow, the sun of curiosity blazed bright causing the ice to melt and rivers of wisdom to flow. Shakti kept asking questions until Shiva broke his silence and revealed how the layers of the body may connect with the layers of the world and become a single fabric, unknotted, uncrumpled, joyful. The serpent around Shiva's neck overheard this conversation that caused him to sprout many heads and hands; he eventually acquired human form and became known as

Yoga secrets revealed

Patanjali and shared this knowledge with the world. This same knowledge was overheard and transmitted by a fish, who became a man called Matsyendra. This same knowledge was carried south by Agastya, who also took with him the mountains and rivers from the north, as well his beautiful wife, the rishika and yogini known as Lopamudra. Saraswati gave this knowledge to Brahma and it was overheard by a goose, who transformed from Hamsa to Param-hamsa when it shared the knowledge with the Sapta Rishis, the seven sages of the celestial sphere, who then shared it with devas as well as asuras. Vishnu shared it with Lakshmi on the ocean of milk. As a fish, he also shared it with Manu, the leader of men. Sita gave this same knowledge to Ram, when he sat on this throne and it was overheard and transmitted by Hanuman. Radha gave it to Krishna, enabling him to let go of Madhu-van and move to Mathura and fulfil his destiny. Krishna, in turn, gave it on the battleground to Arjuna, enabling him to fight without anger in Kurukshetra. The hermit Dattatreya discovered this knowledge everywhere: in rocks and rivers, in trees and animals, in the behaviour of men and of women. So did the Jinas. So did the Buddhas. This knowledge is known as 'yoga'. And these stories, yoga mythology.

Patanjali

Before we delve deeper into yoga mythology, let us first understand what yoga is, and what mythology is.

What is Yoga?

Every day in the morning, women in traditional India use rice flour to create patterns known as kolam or rangoli on the floor just outside their house. Dots are joined with lines, reminding us how connecting stars to create constellations helps us understand the sky. Likewise, connecting data creates information, connecting parts creates the whole, and joining the limited helps us explore the limitless. This household ritual is a metaphor for yoga.

Kolam

The simplest meaning of yoga (often pronounced 'joga' by many Indians) is alignment. This alignment can be between two parts of the body, two objects or two concepts. In Indian astrology, or jyotisha-shastra, for example, when stars and planets are aligned in a particular way to create a beneficial pattern, the word 'yoga' or 'joga' is used to describe it. The same word is used in social contexts for the coming together of seemingly unaligned things to bring about success. A person who aligns things that are seemingly unaligned in order to get things done is deemed 'jugadu', or 'jogadu' (in Odia, a language from east India), which means a resourceful person, though the word is sometimes used pejoratively for a fixer. The yogi, or jogi, and the yogini, or jogini, were those who aligned seemingly misaligned forces to get things done. That is what made a yogi 'yogya', or worthy.

Depending on the context, yoga has come to have different meanings: alignment of the mind with the body, or of breath and mind, or of mind, breath and body, or simply between different body parts. It could be harmony between the front and back, the left and the right sides, or the upper and lower parts of the body. Some might say it is a connection of the individual with society; others, the connection between two human beings, whether husband and wife, parent and child, teacher and student, or friends. In a religious context, one would say it is the connection between the devotee and the deity.

Various adjectives are now used to describe how this connection is achieved. For example, 'karma yoga' deals with connecting through action, where our individual activity is aligned to a larger social goal; 'bhakti yoga' deals with connecting through emotions, with a person or a personal deity; 'gyan yoga' is more intellectual; 'hatha yoga' more physical; 'tantra yoga' favours rituals and symbols.

Patanjali, author of the Yoga-sutra, organized various yogic techniques in a systematic way. His eight-fold (ashtanga) yoga, also known as the royal (raja) yoga, reveals a very traditional Indian understanding of the human body as a series of concentric containers, with the social container (karana sharira) outside the physical (sthula sharira), and the psychological (sukshma sharira) inside the physical. Within the psychological container resides the immortal soul (atma) that

Inner connections

animates us. It is called the resident (dehi) of the body (deha), and is an extension of the boundless container that contains the cosmos (param-atma).

Many use words like 'astral body' for the karana sharira. But this manifests as the social body, which is based on all things we attract to ourselves naturally because of reactions to past actions (karma), or bring into our lives through our present actions (also karma). In Indian mythology, karma is believed to shape the circumstances of our life, both voluntary and involuntary. Also, in Buddhism, the atma is not an eternal entity but a creation of our psychological body. Atma is referred to as 'jiva' in Jainism.

The sequence of eight (ashta) limbs (anga) in the Yoga-sutra becomes a journey from the outside to the inside. So, there is Yama, Niyama, Asana, Pranayama, Pratyahara, Dharana, Dhyana and Samadhi.

Yama deals with social aspects of life, our relationships with others. Niyama is more individualistic, having to do with our relationship with our self. Asanas are the postures that are the most popular visible form of yoga (popular as they can be photographed and are rather dramatic to look at), and

External connections

deal with our body. Pranayama deals with breath. Pratyahara deals with our sense organs through which we connect with the outside world, enabling us to make the journey from the outer world to the inner world. Dharana is about awareness and perspective, letting our thoughts come and go without trying to control them. Dhyana is about focus where we, very consciously and actively, get our mind to concentrate on a single object, thing or idea, like chanting. From Dhyana came words like 'zen' in Japan where yoga spread via Buddhism. Samadhi is the process of connecting with the ultimate.

Relationship of body structure to yogic practices			
Sharira (body)	Kosha (container)	Explanation	Yoga Practice
Karana Sharira (social body)		Relationships	Yama
		Discipline	Niyama
Sthula Sharira (physical body)	Anna	Body	Asana
	Prana	Breath	Pranayama
Sukshma Sharira (psychological body)	Mana	Senses	Pratyahara
	Chitta	Emotions	Dharana
	Buddhi	Intelligence	Dhyana
	Atma	Spirit	Samadhi

But what is the ultimate? For some it means going back to the primal source, the atma within (jiva-atma), which is eternally tranquil (ananda), unfettered by hunger and fear, and inhabiting the body. For others, it is looping back and reconnecting with the atma without: God (param-atma), nature (prakriti), culture (sanskriti).

The word 'samadhi' is also used for the tomb of saints, because saints are believed to have connected with the divine. They don't die; they simply slip out of their body as a sword slips out of a scabbard. Their body is thus pure, untouched by death. Their tombs then become the focal point where you see the connection between the human and the divine worlds.

Samadhi makes yoga rather mystical. But for many, yoga has an occult side too. The practice of yoga bestows upon the yogi magical powers known as 'siddhi', which enable him to change his shape and size, fly in the air,

Yogi seated on a bed of nails

walk on water, grant children to the childless, and defeat demons and witches. Many an Indian folktale speaks of yogis who are at once mystical and deal with the occult. They can voluntarily leave their body, as if it's a shell, travel around the world and to astral realms, and return at will. Siddhi is linked to semen-power, retaining it and reversing its flow up the spine till it sprouts in the brain, an act described in Tantric texts as the uncoiling of the serpent Kundalini and the opening of lotus-wheels or chakras.

Yogic postures have been traced to 4000-year-old clay seals from the Harappan period, which depict a man seated in the throne position (Bhadra-asana). The word 'yoga', however, comes from Vedic scriptures composed over 3000 years ago. Initially, yoga referred to connecting the cart to the horse or the ox. Rishis or seers, who preferred to live

Proto-Shiva on Harappan seal

on the edge of society, and contemplated on the nature of reality, made yoga a metaphor for spiritual practices.

Around 2500 years ago, with the rise of monastic orders

Yoke of a bullock cart

('shramana' in Sanskrit) such as Buddhism and Jainism, the meaning of yoga became more metaphorical as it began to refer to various techniques that enabled monks to break free from the hunger and fear that entraps humans in the wheel of rebirth (samsara). The practice granted oblivion (nirvana) to Buddhists, liberation (moksha) to Hindus, omniscience (kaivalya) to Jains, and supernatural powers (siddhi) to Tantrics of all faiths.

When the Puranic stories of Shiva and Shakti were being composed, around 2000 years ago, the Bhagavad Gita, a dialogue found in the epic Mahabharata, spoke of yoga in devotional and mystical terms. This was later elaborated by

Vedanta scholars as involving the union of the individual soul (jiva-atma) with the cosmic soul (param-atma), an idea that is now being popularized by Indian gurus in the West.

The most popular definition of yoga – chitta vritti nirodha, or unknotting the knots of the mind – was codified about 1500 years ago. It is attributed to Patanjali, whom some see as a historical figure, and others as a mythological figure, as yoga is seen as timeless wisdom, not bound to history or

The self (jiva, atma)

geography. By this time, yoga was linked to tapasya, the practice of churning mental fire (tapa) by hermits. It was also linked to Tantra, occult practices that enabled hermits to control the workings of the cosmos and change the destiny of people. Yoga became not just about wisdom, but also about power.

Nath yogis such as Gorakh-nath who lived around 1000 years ago gave greater emphasis to the physical and the occult side of yoga (siddhi). This was the time when Tantric literature became popular and we find more and more stories of yoginis, who are both enchanting and fearsome. Circular temples with no roofs were built for them, enabling them to fly in and out with ease. Yogis sought to control yoginis who in turn sought to seduce and domesticate them.

Yogini

Mainstream yoga, as we know it today, was formalized around the late nineteenth century when Indians, ruled by the British, were increasingly exposed to popular European fitness regimes based on gymnastics. Yoga came to be associated more with physical health than mental health. In the West, religious orders viewed it with suspicion as an 'Eastern religious practice', forcing yoga teachers to play down its spiritual, mystical, occult and religious angles.

Over the centuries, despite various historical changes, a world view has persisted, first expressed in Vedic hymns, then in Buddhist, Jain, Vedantic and Tantric philosophies, and finally in Puranic, Agamic and Jataka stories. Using fantastic landscape, plots and characters, this world view is presented where time and space are without beginning, without end, and always changing, where death is followed by rebirth endlessly. It separates the mind from matter, spirit from substance, the subtle from the gross, the formless from the form, the self from the other, the limitless from the limited. It speaks of how the mind becomes knotted because of anxiety and fear caused in life, because life frightens us by making demands of us. We have to find food in order to survive, to nourish ourselves; we have to protect ourselves from danger; we are constantly in

Yogi

a state of freeze, fight or flight. We are seeking things and avoiding things. Yoga is a process by which the knots are untied, enabling us to align ourselves with the true nature of the world, not what we imagine it to be. With this insight, we can break free from hunger and fear, and eventually the cycle of rebirths. We can mystically unite with the cosmos or develop occult powers that help us solve human problems.

What is Mythology?

A fact is everybody's truth, based on measurable evidence. Fiction is nobody's truth, based on fantasy. Myth is somebody's truth, and establishes a culture's world view.

The words 'myth' and 'mythology' are controversial only if one sticks to their nineteenth-century definitions, where myth is a synonym of fiction and fantasy. This simplistic binary world has long since collapsed. In the twenty-first century, our understanding of the world is far more nuanced. It must be kept in mind that the meaning of words changes with time. The word 'gay' today refers to homosexuality and not carefree as it did a century ago; for the Greeks 'justice' meant the natural order of hierarchy, not equality as it does today. Myth therefore has to be seen in the modern context, not the colonial one.

The Age of Enlightenment was also the Age of Colonization, a fact that is rarely pointed out. During this age whatever the European colonizers believed in was the truth, and whatever their subjects in Asia, Africa and America said was deemed as falsehood and myth. In the twenty-first century, following the rise of science, we have realized different people

Lady Justice

have different truths, because they have different experiences of the world. European or American truths are also a form of myth constructed through stories, symbols and rituals. Therefore the word 'myth' refers to a subjective or cultural truth of the people.

Myth is not just a religious concept; it is also a secular concept. The two most popular example of myth are God and justice. Some people believe in God, some don't. For believers, God is true, for non-believers God is not true. What about justice? Is it fact, fiction, or just an assumption, hope or belief? Does justice exist? Some people will say justice exists; some that it does not. Again, for the believer, it is true, while for the non-believer it is not true. Neither God nor justice is a universal concept, though many want them to be, assuming that these will make the world a better place.

Myth is an idea and the vehicles that transmit this idea over time and space are stories, symbols and rituals. Mythology is the study of the stories, symbols and rituals that communicate myth. When we decode them in the course of trying to understand the cultural truth of a people, we realize how mythologies change and why myths are different across history and geography.

Every human being lives in myth. This is an important point to remember. A common misconception among people is that modern, civilized people don't live in myth, while primitive people or exotic cultures do. This is not true. The difference between human beings and animals is that human beings seek meaning in life. In order to bring meaning to life, we frame the world in a particular way. We have assumptions about life, death and purpose. Therefore, we tell each other stories and through them construct a world view; this is our myth. Thus, every tribe in the world, whether in Africa or in America, every person living in New York, Mumbai or Tokyo has a particular view of the world: that is the myth he or she lives in. In most cases, these myths are inherited, they are transmitted over generations. However, in the twenty-first century, the respect for inherited traditions is dwindling as our faith in technology rises.

Gradually, we are living in a world of ideologies which are transmitted through educational institutions and social media, and which in turn transmit new myths that are constructed on a day-to-day basis. A tribal society will have a tribal myth, a civilized society will have its own 'civilized' myth. Communism and capitalism are as much a myth as Judaism, Christianity, Islam, Buddhism and Hinduism. The nation state is a myth, too – these are frameworks in which we live. If tribal mythology creates tribal loyalty, nation-state mythology establishes patriotism. Capitalism creates a sense of purpose based on creating value, Communism creates a myth that privileges labour. Everyone who is in a myth, insists that his or her myth is true, and that those who disagree live in falsehood. Money is the most powerful myth in the world today. A coin, a piece of paper or numbers on a computer screen are deemed to have value, because the buyer and the seller believe in the underlying story and respect the symbol and rituals around it. Take away this myth and modern society will collapse.

Just as science rejected myth in the nineteenth century on grounds of evidence, post-structuralists, social justice warriors and cultural Marxists reject all myths of the twenty-first century as conspiracies to create oppression. In their discourses, Capitalism was created to make the rich richer, Communism to establish mediocrity and kill enterprise, Hinduism to enslave people through caste, Christianity to establish empires, Islam to wipe out free will and diversity. All religions are considered tools to create gender, class and cultural hierarchies, to create value for the favoured few. By such analysis, post-structuralists, social justice warriors and cultural Marxists create their own hierarchies and meanings, establishing their own myth of a world without myth.

For the purpose of yoga, it is important to understand the myth of Judgement Day. Judgement Day is a concept that is found in Judaism, Christianity and Islam. It was also found in ancient Egyptian, Persian, Mesopotamian and Greek mythology. The idea is that when you die, you are judged on your actions, and sent to heaven or hell accordingly. In the case of Judaism, Christianity and Islam, God is the judge. And therefore, God creates the rules one must follow. If one follows the rules, they go to heaven or else, hell. Secular nation states also follow the framework underlying Judgement Day, though they exclude the idea of God. Instead of God, they speak of citizens as a collective, and commandments take the form of a constitution. The citizens are expected to live by the nation's law: those who don't are judged and penalized. Structurally, then, the notion of Judgement Day is implicit even in the secular idea of social justice and corporate social responsibility.

The concept of a judge, Judgement Day, and the binary between heaven and hell are not dominant motifs in Hinduism, Buddhism or Jainism. In Buddhism, the Buddha is not a judge. The idea of heaven and hell exists, but is not quite based on judgement or commandments. Buddhism speaks of the concept of karma and the belief in rebirth, based on your actions in this life. The rules of Hinduism, Buddhism and Jainism are restricted to religious ascetic orders and communities, more for functional than metaphysical reasons. You go to heaven not by following rules but by restraining senses and seeking wisdom. Thus, the Buddhist concept of heaven and hell is not based on following or breaking rules, but on psychological transformation, and accumulating karma that either raises us or casts us down in the many-tiered cosmos.

Judgement Day

The concept of judgement comes in a society that believes in equality, and therefore strives towards homogeneity, shunning heterogeneity. Hinduism, Buddhism and Jainism are based on diversity which is often misread as inequality. Every human being is different, because we all carry different karmic burdens from our previous lives. Each one has different strengths and weaknesses, opportunities and threats. So, one rule cannot apply to all. Likewise, different people need different forms of yoga and different kinds of teachers. There is no one yoga for all, no one guru for all. The yoga that works for our particular context and our body, is best for us, but might not work for others. Yoga cannot be benchmarked or indexed or standardized. Nor can gurus, yogis or yoginis.

Contrasting Worldviews	
Abrahamic mythology	**Indic mythology**
Monotheistic	Monotheistic, polytheistic, agnostic
Equality	Diversity
Time is linear and finite	Time is cyclical and infinite
One life	Many lives
Obedience	Awareness
Be saved or judged	Be liberated or united

What is Yoga Mythology?

Yoga postures have been given different names of Indian origin, such as Vira-asana, Svana-asana, Manjara-asana, Galava-asana, Surya-namaskar. Some of these are easily translated as the Hero pose, Dog pose, Cat pose, but some are proper nouns and make sense only if you are familiar with Hindu mythology. Some names may describe a pose, as they mimic an animal, as in the Dog or Cat pose, which may or may not refer to a deity's sacred animal or mount (vahana). Some names for poses can also be random labels that create a sense of the exotic, and carry a stamp of authenticity. Some believe the names directly identify the yogi who invented the pose, such as Ruchika-asana (the pose of Ruchika), or are instructing people to develop a particular attitude, such as Virabhadra-asana (the Righteous Warrior pose). By seeking out the stories underlying the names one gets a sense of Indian mythology in which yoga was nurtured over thousands of years. This book aims to present those stories in a systematic way, so that readers can enjoy not just the stories but also appreciate the underlying philosophy.

This book uses various yoga postures as inspiration to leap into the world of Hindu mythology, with occasional detours into Jain and Buddhist mythology. These three mythologies that emerged from the Indian subcontinent are all based on the concept of rebirth, and all three of them value yoga as a technology that prepares the body to realize its highest physical, psychological, emotional, intellectual, mystical and occult potential.

In Hindu mythology, the word 'tapasya' is often used interchangeably with yoga. Tapasya means churning of tapa,

or mental fire, to burn the knots of the mind, and throw light on the mystical and occult secrets of the universe. Various gods, demons, sages and humans perform tapasya to invoke gods and change the world and their life. Bhagirath, a prince of the solar dynasty, does tapasya until he is able to get the celestial river Mandakini to flow down on earth as the river Ganga. Mahisha, an asura, performs tapasya until he gets the boon that he cannot be killed by man, god, demon,

Fire-ascetic and water-nymph

mineral, plant or animal (he forgets to include women on the list, and is eventually slain by Durga).

The greatest threat to the tapasvin, the one who churns mental fire, is the celestial damsel known as apsara. She tempts him and causes him to lose control of his senses and spurt out semen, a popular metaphor for loss of mental control. If tapa refers to fire and tapasvin to the fire-ascetic, then apsa refers to water and apsara to the water-nymph. The tension between the two is the tension between our body and the temptations that end up knotting our mind. It is the same tension seen between Siddhartha Gautama and the demon of desire, Mara, in Buddhist mythology. After defeating Mara, Siddhartha Gautama becomes the Buddha. In Nath-yogi mythology, the celibate yogis shun the enchanting yoginis who seek to entrap them in the enchanted banana orchard.

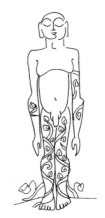

Jain monk

Sadly, these stories are often taken literally and women are seen as embodiments of temptation. The female biology was seen as incapable of reaching the highest levels of spiritual growth. For that, it was believed women would have to be reborn with a male body, one that produces semen whose flow can be restrained and reversed through yoga. In Sukhavati, the pure land, the heaven of enlightened beings in Mahayana Buddhism, every resident is male, born not from a woman's womb but from a lotus flower. In Jainism too, the most aware beings, the Jinas, are all male.

Tapasya is effort (shrama) and so tapasvins are also called shramanas, though this word is often restricted to Buddhist and Jain monks. Yoga, or tapasya, is seen as the tool to achieve omniscience (kaivalya) in Jain tradition, oblivion (nirvana) in Buddhist tradition, liberation through union with the divine

Buddha

(moksha) in Hindu tradition, and siddhi (occult powers) in Tantric traditions of Jainism, Buddhism and Hinduism. And so, all holy men of India were seen as yogis (or jogis in local parlance), and holy women as yoginis (or as the restrained jogan, or the wild jogini in folklore). Yogis and yoginis are also known as gosain and gosani, masters of the cow, a common Indian metaphor for the senses that 'graze on the pasture' of external stimuli.

People often wonder where the various yoga positions came from. Most of the positions we see today are about a hundred years old, designed in the royal courts of India, influenced by European gymnasiums. But in traditional Hindu lore, the yogis of India have been practicing these positions for thousands of years. That is what gave them insights into the world and made them not only healthy and wise, but also granted them supernatural powers known as siddhi. In mythology, this wisdom comes from nature, from plants and animals, and the gods, seers and ascetics, some of whom were more powerful than the gods.

The modern obsession with specialization and expertise assumes that yoga was known only to yogis; but in ancient times, this kind of classification did not exist. In the past, the philosopher was also an alchemist, a sorcerer, a storyteller, a shaman, a problem-solver, a teacher, a coach, a psychiatrist and a doctor. Similarly, yogis were also seen as experts in medicine, mysticism, astrology and the occult, as well as various art forms, from painting to singing to dancing. For instance, Shiva, the yogi, is also Nataraja, the lord of dance and theatre. It is known that many soldiers of ancient India exercised through dance. Dance helped the soldiers remain fit and focused and work together as teams. It also kept them entertained. And through dance, stories of gods were shared. Many of the gestures that we see in yoga today probably originated from these dance steps.

Asanas are usually divided into those that focus on stillness and those that focus on movement. Postures that promote meditation were popular amongst the yogis who would sit still in one position and spend their time observing, meditating and contemplating on the mysteries of the universe. Dynamic postures came from the yoginis who were also dancers. A circle of dancing yoginis is an integral part of traditional Hindu temples. Ironically, the contribution of women to yoga has been largely ignored. India has a vast oral tradition and the reliance on textual evidence restricts our knowledge to the written word of elite groups dominated by men. Since, for these male writers, Shiva is the primal yogi and his students are also male, they conveniently overlook the primal yogini, Shakti, and her companions, some of whom form the female collective of Matrikas and Mahavidyas. Parvati, the princess of the mountains,

Yogini

was Shakti, the primal yogini who made Shiva reveal the secrets of yoga in words as well as through postures. The words were documented by Patanjali in his Yoga-sutra, and the gestures by Bharata in his Natyashastra. We remember the male God, the male scholars and the male gurus, but we forget the Goddess and the independent women – ganikas, devadasis and natis who nurtured India's dance tradition in temples, until they were abused as 'prostitutes' in the puritanical Victorian era and completely sidelined.

The sources of Yoga mythology are mostly oral. But there are many textual versions too. In India, writing became common only 2300 years ago, after the reign of King Ashoka, who used the Brahmi script to write his edicts. From linguistic analysis, we know that the oldest hymns are the Vedas, which are over 3000 years old. Then came the Upanishads, which are over 2500 years old and full of metaphysical and philosophical content. Then came the epics Ramayana and Mahabharata, about 2000 years ago, and chronicles known as the Puranas, which are about 1500 years old.

Buddhist stories come from the Jatakas which were put down in writing at the same time as the Hindu epics. Jain stories come from the Jain Puranas and Jain retellings of the Ramayana and the Mahabharata, which are as old as Buddhist tales, but were put down in writing much later, about 1000 years ago.

Hindu texts were composed mostly in Sanskrit. Jains and Buddhists chose to write in Prakrit and Pali, though later Mahayana Buddhists and Jain acharyas switched to Sanskrit. In the last 1000 years, many of these stories have been retold in regional languages as songs and ballads, orally transmitted by bards and performers, as well as visualized on temple walls as sculptures, frescoes and murals.

Faith	Story source	Content
Hindu	Vedas	Collection of hymns and rituals to Vedic deities
Hindu	Ramayana	Story of Ram, greatest king of the solar dynasty
Hindu	Mahabharata	Story of the war between the Pandavas and Kauravas of the lunar dynasty
Hindu	Puranas	Story of the Hindu trinity (male and female)
Buddhist	Jatakas	Rebirth stories of the Buddha-to-be
Jain	Trisasti-salaka-purusha-charitra	Stories of 63 great men who appear in every eon

In the eighteenth century, European Orientalists privileged Sanskrit, which Hindus consider to be the language of the gods, equating it with Latin. They also privileged texts over orality. That is why the history of yoga is often sought through textual traditions, an idea that makes little sense to Hindus, who prefer the words of their gurus, the teachers and transmitters of living knowledge. For Hindus, Buddhists and Jains, yoga has always been part of their history as their mythologies constantly refer to yogis and yoginis, tapasvis and tapasvinis, gosains and gosanis; some of these were restrained sages while others were wild sorcerers.

Enjoy the stories in this book as they have been enjoyed by Hindus over the ages, seeking not logic, but the wisdom that forms the foundation of yoga.

Structure of the book

There are manuscripts dating back to the tenth and fifteenth centuries which refer to eighty-four yoga poses. For Hindus, these postures come from the gods and there have been many variations, introduced by many gurus, over time. The god Shiva came up with 84,000 poses, based on 84,000 living creatures, of which eighty-four were received by various yogis and yoginis, which were then transmitted to humanity. Now, 84,000 is a mythical number to indicate comprehensiveness; for example, in Buddhist literature, it is said that Buddha gave 84,000 different lessons, for 84,000 different kinds of beings, to suit their needs, and his relics were distributed across 84,000 locations.

Chess board

In the last 100 years, yoga gurus have devised somewhere between 100 to 300 poses. In this book, we focus only on sixty-four poses. Why just

Yoginis face inward in roofless Tantric temples

sixty-four? Because the number sixty-four, like eighty-four, indicates infinity. Eight refers to the cardinal and the ordinal directions in two dimensions. In three dimensions, there are eight multiplied by eight, sixty-four directions.

Also, the game of chess played with sixty-four squares was invented in India, and later travelled with Arabs to Persia and thence Europe. The man who invented it gave it to a king in exchange for a few grains of rice: 1 for the first square, 2 for the second, 4 for the third, and so on. So for the entire board he needed 2^{63} grains of rice, which works out to over 18 billion tonnes of rice. Infinite rice, for the king at least.

In Tantric lore, the number sixty-four refers to all the knowledge of the world, embodied as sixty-four vidyas or

Yoginis face outward in roofed Vedantic temples

Brahma, the creator

Vishnu, the preserver

Shiva, the destroyer

yoginis that yogis invoke or seek to capture. Thirty-two of these yoginis can transform a man into a king, sixty-four into a yogi. There are many temples in India where sixty-four yoginis are depicted as forming a circle of power. In circular Tantric temples, which have no roof, they face inside and are the main deities. In Agamic or Vedantic temples, they face outside, and the space behind them is where the deity is enshrined.

The sixty-four yoga poses that are discussed in this book have been classified into four sections: Devi, Brahma, Vishnu and Shiva, the four pillars of Hindu mythology. This classification is arbitrary, based on stories and not sequencing of asanas. Devi, the female form of the divine, is complemented by the three male forms of the divine: Brahma, Vishnu and Shiva.

Devi embodies prakriti, the material, measurable part of the world; she embodies nature too. Many mythologies see nature as feminine, hence the English phrase Mother Nature. In Hindu mythology, culture is also feminine. Culture is domesticated nature, so the Goddess has two forms, the wild Kali and the domesticated Gauri, from whom emerge Lakshmi, the goddess of wealth, and Saraswati, the goddess of knowledge. Devi is also known as Shakti or Durga, as she is essentially power.

Brahma, Vishnu and Shiva embody purusha, the human response to material reality. Brahma, Vishnu and Shiva are referred to as the creator, preserver and destroyer but what they create, preserve and destroy is culture, not nature. Hence, Devi is their mother, and simultaneously the daughter of Brahma, the sister of Vishnu and the wife of Shiva. Brahma seeks to control nature as he creates culture, which makes him unworthy of worship. Shiva rejects all control, of culture and nature, and so is the hermit, until Shakti coaxes him to be a householder. Vishnu is the enlightened householder. Unlike the hermit Shiva, Vishnu engages with nature and culture, and unlike the unenlightened householder Brahma, he does not seek to control nature or culture, but connects with the Goddess at a responsible level, with love. Notice how God is equated with verbs (create, sustain, destroy) and Goddess with nouns (wealth, power, knowledge) indicating how together they embody subject and object and create language.

Saraswati, knowledge

Lakshmi, wealth

Durga, power

A Hindu yogi's journey

Since they arose from the same cultural matrix, Buddhist and Jain mythologies have many things in common with Hindu mythology, but there are stark differences as well. All three believe in the wheel of rebirth and none have concepts such as evil or Judgement Day. Buddhism does not have the concept of a soul or God. Jainism believes in souls within individual beings but has no concept of a cosmic soul or God. In Hinduism, the cosmic soul manifests as matter (Devi) and mind (Brahma, Vishnu and Shiva), and every one of us is a diminutive double of that cosmic soul, with the potential to return to the primal unknotted state.

A Jain yogi's journey

Shiva's hermit form (not his householder form) has much in common with the Buddha and the Jina. The ultimate aim in Buddhism and Jainism, is to become a hermit. Hinduism, however, values a return to the household as a hermit–householder, engaged in duties but detached from desires.

A Buddhist yogi's journey

In Theravada Buddhism, the Buddha walks out of his role as king, son, father and husband. In Mahayana Buddhism, the Bodhisattva delays his rise to Buddhahood until he saves all suffering souls.

Yoga Mythology: 64 Asanas and Their Stories

Distinguishing features of Indic mythologies			
	Individual Soul (part of God) Jiva-atma Jiva Atma	Cosmic Soul (all of God) Param-atma Bhagavan Ishwar Brahman	Highest Value
Buddhism	Absent	Absent	Hermit
Jainism	Present	Absent	Hermit
Hinduism	Present	Present	Hermit-householder

In Jainism, the Jina or Tithankara, having lived previous lives as a Vasudeva (hero) and Chakravarti (king, or leader), and a current life as a householder, renounces everything, including his clothes and his identity. This is why these all-seeing sages look the same on temple walls, distinguished only by symbols.

In Hinduism, wisdom makes the still Shiva descend from his mountain abode of Kailas and become a householder of Kashi, and the sleeping Vishnu rises up from the ocean of milk and descends to earth as Ram and Krishna, his mortal avatars. God (param-atma) descends, or manifests in form, to uplift the individual self (jiva-atma) into wisdom.

At the heart of wisdom is a better understanding of the Goddess, hence the yoginis, so that we dance with her rather than seek control over her.

As you read the sixty-four stories of the sixty-four postures, across the four sections, you will enter the wonderful world of Indic mythology, mostly Hindu but with occasional detours into Buddhism and Jainism.

Devi	Brahma	Shiva	Vishnu
Surya	Omkar	Parvata	Ananta
Ardha Chandra	Hamsa	Siddha	Garuda
Purvottana	Marichi	Bhairava	Mala
Paschimottana	Vasishtha	Svana	Chakra
Vriksha	Durvasa	Virabhadra	Bala
Padma	Ruchika	Nataraja	Matsya
Baka	Vishwamitra	Shava	Nava
Krauncha	Galava	Skanda	Kurma
Kakka	Ashtavakra	Shanmukha	Varaha
Kukkuta	Kaundinya	Mayura	Simha
Gomukha	Kashyapa	Gaja	Ganda Bherunda
Vrischika	Vajra	Matsyendra	Trivikrama
Manjara		Goraksha	Bhadra
Makara		Danda	Setu Bandha
Bhujanga			Hanuman
Bheka			Tola
Dhanur			Hala
Pasha			Bhuja Pida
			Vatayana
			Pinda

Devi

Without the Goddess, there cannot be God. This is one of the many differences between Hindu mythology and Judeo-Christian-Islamic mythology (aka Abrahamic or Semitic mythology), which emerged in the Near and Middle East and spread all over the world.

The Bible describes how God created the world, and how the world will come to an end with the Apocalypse. Christians and Muslims believe in Judgement Day when all human beings will be made answerable for their actions on earth in the one life they lived: were they in accordance with God's law? By contrast, in Hindu mythology, the world has no beginning or end: it has always existed, sometimes with form, and sometimes without. God is not

Lakshmi, wealth

33

a creator. Also, we live not one life but infinite lives, our current life being determined by past lives and future lives being determined by our actions in this life. In other words, in Hindu mythology, God is not a judge. The world is a self-sustaining entity visualized as the Goddess. She has always existed. But she is 'seen' when God awakens. God here does not mean someone outside creation; God is the ability to be aware, hence 'create' the world. If Jews, Christians and Muslims pray to God for the food He provides; Hindus pray to food as God.

We must clarify here that gender in Hindu mythology is used as a metaphor and must not be taken literally. Unfortunately, the human mind tends to take things literally and, when we speak of the Goddess, we assume we are speaking about women, and when we speak of God, that we are speaking about men. However, that is not correct. Our body has a physical side and a psychological side. The physical side of our body is the Goddess and the psychological side of our body is God. As we all know, the physical and psychological sides are closely related to each other. We can always ask what comes first: the physical or the psychological? But we will find it a very difficult question to answer. Similarly, it is very difficult to answer: Does the Goddess come first or God?

According to scientists, the world began 13 billion years ago with the Big Bang. The earth came into being about 5 billion years ago, and about 4 billion years ago, life

Durga, power

emerged. What we mean by 'life' is a psychological response to the physical world. For the first time, we see micro-organisms that possess the instinct to survive, that are seeking nourishment, nutrition and food to sustain themselves. Humans appeared only 1,00,000 years ago: they had the power to imagine. They controlled fire

Saraswati, knowledge and the arts

and water and reshaped the environment to create villages and cities, something no other animal had done before.

Technically, from a scientific point of view, we can see the world existed before life emerged; the physical existed before the psychological. In the Hindu scheme of things, the world would be called the Goddess and that which creates life would be called God. More correctly, God's arrival is mapped not to the arrival of life but to the arrival of humans, with the power of imagination, for of all animals humans alone can observe and reflect on nature, and even find ways to controlling nature and improve on it. This awakening of the human is the arrival of God. These complex ideas are presented in Hindu mythology using the metaphors of gender.

In some scriptures, the Goddess is described as a mother and in others, as a daughter, a wife and a sister. These are metaphors to inform us that nature pre-dates all things and so she is the mother. Humans create culture by domesticating nature. Culture is then the daughter, wife or sister of humanity, depending on how we engage with culture.

The main difference between Hinduism and monastic religions like Buddhism and Jainism is the value placed on the Goddess. Monasticism seeks freedom from culture first, and then nature. They wish to break free from the Goddess, from desire and fear. They give up family and all connections with society. In the quest for tranquillity and equanimity they struggle against desire, and against death to attain immortality. While in Buddhism, Siddhartha Gautama walks out on his wife to become the Buddha, and in Jainism, all Jinas walk out of family life after completing family obligations, in Hinduism, the great Shiva who destroys hunger and fear is asked by the Goddess to voluntarily submit to marriage and household. In Mahayana Buddhism, Tara and the many yoginis exist to help the sage make the journey towards oblivion (nirvana, shunya). In Jainism, the yoginis and the yakshis serve only as guardians to the Jina.

With this background, let us now move to the asanas associated with or inspired by the Goddess. In this section,

you will read about things that are mostly related to nature: space, time, plants and animals. Many animals will be found in other sections as well as they are more meaningful in the context of Brahma, Vishnu and Shiva. But typically, this section talks about nature in all its glory, without human intervention.

Yogini

1

Surya Namaskar
Bowing to the Sun

The earliest images of the sun come to us from Buddhist art where he is shown on a chariot with his wives or female archers by his side, shooting arrows, driving away the darkness of the night. In Hindu temples, the sun-god Surya is depicted riding a chariot with seven horses, indicating the seven days of the week. Each of the twelve wheels of the chariot represents one month of the year; and the eight spokes in each wheel indicate the traditional divisions of the day. He is accompanied by his wives, Sanjana and Chhaya. His charioteer is the dawn god, who is sometimes visualized as the male Aruni and sometimes as the female Usha. In the Upanishads, it is the sun who reveals to sage Yagnavalkya,

Surya's chariot

deprived of Vedic wisdom by his teacher, that in us, and in everything around us, is the divine potential (Brahman) to expand the mind and realize infinity.

The sun also taught Hanuman, who designed the Surya Namaskar as a way of thanking his guru.

Hanuman is a very important character in the Hindu epic Ramayana, which was composed over 2000 years ago. It retells the ancient story of how Ram, a prince of Ayodhya who was exiled to a forest, rescues his wife, Sita, from Ravana, the demon-king of the island of Lanka. Ram is helped by a monkey army that builds a bridge across the sea. Hanuman is the general of this army, but he is no ordinary monkey. In him the divine potential is fully realized, especially after his interaction with Ram, who is a mortal form of the immortal Vishnu.

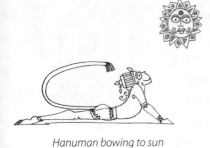

Hanuman bowing to sun

As a child, Hanuman was so strong that he jumped to the sky to eat the rising sun, thinking it was a golden fruit. When he grew up, he wanted to learn everything about the world, and he asked his mother how he

could achieve his objective. His mother pointed to the sky and said that the sun sees everything and maybe he should talk to him. Hanuman went to Surya and said he wanted to learn everything that the sun god saw and everything that he had observed of the world. Surya, however, said that he had no time to teach, since he travelled all day and rested all night; he would not be able to pause even for a moment for Hanuman. You don't have to pause, said Hanuman. He decided to ride in front of the sun's chariot each day so that Surya could teach him while they were travelling. The sun god warned that his glare would be unbearable and the pain and heat would be intolerable. Hanuman replied that it did not matter, for knowledge cannot come without some suffering, one must work hard to acquire it. Impressed by his determination, Surya agreed and that is how Hanuman was educated. He spent thousands of years staring at the sun from sunrise to sunset, listening to everything that the sun had to say. Immersed in knowledge, he realized his divine potential. He transformed from Hanuman, the monkey, with finite knowledge and strength, to Hanuman, the god, with infinite wisdom and power. He thanked his teacher and expressed his gratitude by designing the Surya Namaskar.

Possibly the most well-known sequence of asanas, the Surya Namaskar, literally, 'Bowing to the Sun', is incorporated into the beginning of many styles of asana practice. Each movement is done on an intentional inhale or exhale based on the position to which the practitioner is transitioning, giving it a rather fluid and natural appearance. Many variations of this sequence exist, and as many as 108 repetitions can be counted depending on the particular discipline. The variation depicted here is one of the most commonly known, originating from the Ashtanga Vinyasa method of Mysore, and it serves as the foundational basis for many vinyasa styles of asana practice. Interestingly enough, the Sanskrit word 'vinyasa' comes from the conjunction of 'nyasa', which means 'to put' or 'to place', and the prefix 'vi-', which implies 'in a special or particular way'. Together, vinyasa literally translates to 'order', 'sequence' or 'progression', giving rise to the more dynamic approaches of the physical practice. In keeping with its name, this sequence is traditionally done facing east towards the rising sun.

2

Ardha Chandra-asana
The Half-moon Pose

The sun and the moon represent day and night and so complete time. They are visualized as hairpins of the Goddess whose hair stretches out as the sky.

The moon, known as Chandra or Soma, is a romantic god. He rose from the ocean of milk. He is the most handsome of all the gods and is considered the epitome of male beauty. He is associated in astrology with emotions, romantic desires and moodiness. Like Surya, he too rides a chariot, drawn by antelopes in Hindu iconography, and by geese in Tantric Buddhist iconography.

Chandra's chariot

Typically, Chandra is depicted as a crescent, to distinguish him from the sun. The crescent form is that of a waning moon, not the waxing moon. This has to do with the strained relationship between Chandra and his wives, the constellations known as Nakshatras.

In Western mythology, according to the zodiac system, the sky is divided into twelve parts, based on twelve constellations. In Hindu mythology, the sky is divided into twenty-eight parts, based on twenty-eight different constellations, one of which is supposed to have disappeared. These Nakshatras are visualized as goddesses. The moon god was their common husband, but he preferred only one of his wives, which is why the twenty-eighth wife disappeared. The other twenty-six complained to their father who got so angry with the moon god for favouring one wife over the others that he cursed him with tuberculosis – kshaya-roga or wasting disease. The moon started to wane and he kept waning. Just when he was about to disappear, he prayed to the great god Shiva, who created so much energy within himself through the practice of yoga that he could give some to the moon to start waxing again. The half-moon or the crescent shape of the waning phase of the moon, known as Ardha-chandra, is thus a very important symbol in Hindu mythology. It represents the moment

Goddess with the sun and moon in her hair

between death and rebirth, as well as Shiva's power. Shiva is often described as the god with the crescent moon on his locks.

In another story, the moon god fell in love with the wife of the planet Brihaspati, or

Jupiter, the guru of the devas, gods of the sky. Brihaspati was an old man, very serious and rational; he lacked Chandra's passion. Brihaspati's wife, Tara, meaning 'star', found Chandra very attractive. Bored with Brihaspati, she eventually eloped with Chandra. This led to a crisis in the heavenly kingdoms because Brihaspati went to Indra, the king of the sky, and warned that he would withdraw his support from the devas and not conduct any rituals for them if his wife was not brought back. If Brihaspati did not perform any rituals for the devas, they were doomed to face defeat in battle. Indra was left with no choice. He fought Chandra and forced him to let Tara go.

But when Tara returned home, she was pregnant and everybody wondered whose child it was – her lover Chandra's or her husband Brihaspati's? Tara refused to say anything. When asked, the child in the womb revealed that he was a love child, born of the moon god. An enraged Brihaspati cursed the child: he would be born as neither male nor female.

At birth, this androgynous being was called Budh or Mercury, the child of the star goddess and the moon god. And therefore, Mercury is changeable, neither this nor that, both male and female.

Budh, who is neither male nor female, went

Shiva with the moon in his hair

around the world looking for a wife and found one who was both male and female. Her name was Ila, a prince who entered an enchanted grove and turned into a woman. He begged Shiva and Shakti to remove this enchantment, but all they could do was modify it: he would be male when the moon waxed and female when the moon waned. The descendants of Budh and Ila came to be known as the lunar dynasty.

The kings of India often legitimized their rule by tracing their ancestry to either the sun (the solar dynasty) or the moon (the lunar dynasty). The epic Ramayana tells the story of the former while the epic Mahabharata is the tale of the latter. The solar kings were seen as radiant and upright as the sun, while the lunar kings were seen as moody and shifty like the moon.

Jains believe that the world is without beginning or end, like Jain wisdom. It goes through cycles (kalpas) of good times and bad times. Each kalpa or eon witnesses the arrival of twenty-four Jinas who re-discover Jain wisdom on how to

Jina Chandraprabha

liberate the soul from flesh, how to attain immortality and infinite wisdom from mortality and finite knowledge. A Jina is also known as Tirthankara, the ford-finder, for he finds the path out of material bondage and rebirth. The Jina shares Jain wisdom with the rest of humanity. When he attains supreme wisdom through practice of yoga, his form becomes indistinguishable from other Jinas. So followers associate every Jina with a symbol for the purpose of identification. In this eon, the eighth Jina was Chandraprabha, whose symbol was the crescent moon.

Chandra is the name of the moon. Ardha is the Sanskrit word for 'half' and is used in a lot of asana names. Usually it implies that there is a paripurna, or 'full', variation of the posture, but not so in this case. This pose is meant to represent the balance between shifts in the phases of the moon, and it can be a rather complicated posture to find one's balance in. A common mistake that new practitioners make when working on this asana is to stare at the ground when getting into the position. And while it would seem counter-intuitive to not look at the ground when trying to balance on one leg, since this posture relies on a stacked vertical orientation of the hips, turning the head to look down tends to cause this alignment to falter. This in turn causes the practitioner to lose their balance. Keeping the gaze straight ahead on a fixed point until balance is achieved often makes this posture more accessible and considerably less cumbersome.

3

Purvottana-asana
Stretch of the East

In traditional Hindu rituals, the gods face east so that the light of the rising sun falls on them, and the devotee faces west. However, when doing yoga or performing Vedic rituals, the fire altar is placed in the east and one faces the rising sun.

Most Hindus begin their day facing the sun and pouring water in its direction. Temples across India are designed so that the rising sun's rays fall on the resident deity on particular days, which are seen as especially auspicious.

Directions play a very important role in Hindu, Jain and Buddhist mythologies. From Vedic times, different directions have been given different attributes. The east is

Yagna facing east

Left is north, right is south

associated with the rising sun, and thus growth; the west is associated with the sea, the source from where all things rise and where all things return; the south with death, and thus instability and mortality; and the north with the pole star, hence stability or immortality.

When one is facing the east (purva), one's back is towards the west (paschim), the left hand is to the north (uttara) and the right hand is to the south. Hence, the north is called the left (vama) and the right is called south (dakshina).

The north is the abode of Shiva. As one who teaches the yoga of immortality, he faces south and so is also called Dakshina-murti. The south is where the Goddess comes from, making us aware of material impermanence, and so she is called Dakshina-Kali. The right-handed path, Dakshina-patha, refers to mainstream restrained Vedic rituals. The left-hand path, Vama-patha, refers to subversive sensory Tantric rituals.

In Shiva temples, the leaf-shaped trough points to the north: so when we enter the

Shiva Dakshina-murti

temple, and face the east-facing Shiva-linga, the trough points to our right. Thus the circular pillar of Shiva with no particular orientation is given a direction by the trough, symbol of Shakti.

The back faces the west, whose lord is Varuna, god of the sea and father of Lakshmi, the goddess of fortune. The east is the abode of Indra, who brings rain – transforming the potential of the sea to moisten the parched earth and replenish wells, ponds, lakes and rivers.

Shiva-linga and yogi facing east, pointing north

The Purvottana-asana is derived from purva, the Sanskrit word for 'east'. Since yoga is traditionally practised facing the east, the 'east' side of the body is then the front side, and all together, this asana translates to a 'stretch of the east' pose. Despite the simple appearance of this posture, it actually requires a great deal of core and leg strength to achieve a high lift of the hips. Working towards the full expression of the posture can be done by bending the knees and holding a reverse 'table-top' position, then gradually extending and straightening the legs forward.

———————————

4

Paschimottana-asana
Stretch of the West

Our face or front represents the eastern direction in yoga, our back the west, the left the north and the right the south. In Hindu, Buddhist and Jain mythologies, each of these directions has guardians, Digga-palas.

Broadly, Hindu mythology has two phases: the Vedic and the Puranic. In the Vedas, in ritual manuals that are nearly 3000 years old, six guardians are listed: Agni and Indra of the east, Varuna of the west, Yama of the south, Soma of the north and Brihaspati of the zenith. By the time temples started being built in India for Puranic gods such as Shiva and Vishnu, about 1000 years ago, we find the number of Digga-palas increasing to ten. The ordinal

Back to the west

directions and many old Vedic gods are replaced by Puranic gods. Kubera becomes the lord of the north, replacing Soma. Brahma, instead of Brihaspati, is master of the zenith and the serpent Sesha makes his appearance as the master of the base. The ordinal directions are represented by the moon (the north-east), the sun (the south-west), fire (the north-west) and wind (the south-east).

In Buddhist mythology, across China, Japan and Thailand, one comes upon the Chaturmaharajikas, four kings who stand in the four cardinal directions and guard the Buddha. They are Vaishravana or Kubera, king of the yakshas (hoarders), who guards the north; Dhritarashtra, king of the gandharvas (celestial musicians), who guards the east; Virudhaka, king of the kumbhandas (pot-bellied gnomes), who guards the south; and Virupaksha, king of the nagas (serpents), who guards the west. This idea spread to China via Buddhism and merged with Chinese lore where the four directions are identified with four mythical creatures located as constellations in the sky: a dragon in the east, a white tiger in the west, a turtle in the north and a red bird or phoenix in the south.

These ideas are part of the Indic Vastu-shastra and Chinese Feng-shui, or geomancy, which are used by many people when designing their homes. In Jain mythology, the great re-discoverer of Jain doctrine, the Jina, shares his discovery in all four directions. In every eon, this discovery happens twenty-four times,

Chatur-mukha

which is why every eon has twenty-four Jinas. This act of communication of Jain wisdom to all is called Samavasarana (the refuge to all). Those receiving the knowledge sit around the Jina and speak in all four directions. It reminds us that we are all limited to one direction in our vision; only the Jina who sits in Siddha-loka has access to limitless vision in every direction. This is expressed by making four images of the same Jina, standing back-to-back, facing the four directions, and placing it in a temple that has four entrances (chaturmukha-basadi). This idea of a sage or god facing four directions simultaneously was adopted by Buddhists and Hindus too and it spread across the sea to South East Asia, to places like Pagana in Burma and Angkor Wat in Cambodia where shrines are oriented in all four directions.

In Sanskrit, paschima means 'west' and uttana implies an 'intense stretch'. Together, this asana translates into 'stretch of the west' pose. Traditionally, the practice of this asana is done facing the east (towards the rising sun), so the back becomes the 'west' side of the body, and therefore, this posture could also be referred to as the 'back stretching' pose. There is often confusion about the correct spelling of this, and other asana names, due to the combining of the final 'a' sound in paschima and the 'u' sound in uttana. In Sanskrit, when words are combined, they follow a special set of euphonic blending rules called 'sandhi'. In this case, the 'a' and the 'u' merge to form the long vowel sound 'o'. Regardless of the spelling, this pose is often incorporated in the initial seated portion of asana practices as it is a rather gentle, gravity-assisted stretch of the legs and back.

5

Vriksha-asana
The Tree Pose

Vriksha, or tree, plays a very important role in Hindu, Buddhist and Jain mythologies. In ancient India, as today, trees were associated with gods, holy men and beings known as yakshas and yakshis, and worshipped. Tree worship has been traced to the Harappan civilization, where images of pipal trees being venerated have been found on clay seals. In Buddhism, the pipal tree is sacred as it is under this tree that Buddha became the awakened one, aware of dhamma, the ultimate truth of the world. In some of the earliest examples of Buddhist art, Buddha was often represented as a tree. While Buddha's tree is famous, what is not widely known is that, in Jainism, each and every Jina who finds a way to break free from the material world meditates under a particular tree. Each of the twenty-four Jinas in every eon has a tree associated with them. The first Jina of this eon was Rishabha-nath, who sat under the banyan tree.

In Hinduism too, every god is associated with a tree. Shiva sits under the banyan tree and is offered bilva sprigs; Vishnu

Tulsi (holy basil)

is associated with the kadamba tree and the tulsi bush; the Goddess with tamarind groves and neem trees; and the god of love, Kamadeva, with the mango tree. Indra, king of the devas, has a garden called Nandan-kanan where stands the wish-fulfilling tree or Kalpa-vriksha. Shiva and Shakti enjoy each other's company in the cedar forest or Daru-vana. Hanuman loves the banana forest, or Kadali-vana. Ganesha prefers the sugarcane-forest, or Ikshu-vana. Krishna enjoys the fragrant basil forest, Vrinda-vana, and the sweet fragrant grove known as Madhu-vana.

There are many stories associated with how plants came into being. One story is that they rose when Brahma plucked his hair and placed it on the earth goddess. In Vedic mythology, the goddess Shakambari is known as the mother of plants. In Brahmana literature, the earth goddess was submerged in the sea until Prajapati took the form of a boar, lifted her out of the sea on his snout, and

Tree yakshi

placed her on the back of a turtle. In doing so, his mighty tusks pierced her body and impregnated her with the seeds of plants. In Puranic literature, it is Vishnu who takes the form of a boar, not Prajapati.

Vriksha

In classical Sanskrit poetry, the laughter of women is responsible for the blooming of plants, which is why women were invited to the royal gardens in spring to sing and dance and play. Even in Buddhist art, one finds nymphs holding the branches of trees, smiling and dancing. These are ancient fertility images associated with prosperity and fecundity.

A fundamental balance asana, this posture helps to develop the small muscles in the feet and legs used in maintaining an upright standing position.

Additionally, this pose offers a nice hip-opening stretch in the raised leg. Since gravity is always acting on us in the direction that is perpendicular to the ground, the longer and straighter the body is kept, the easier it is to find and maintain a balanced position. Practitioners who find difficulty balancing in this posture are reminded to distribute their weight evenly across the standing foot; pressing down firmly with the big toe is a simple way of ensuring that this weight distribution is maintained and sustainable. Finally, finding a fixed point on which to lock the gaze can help prevent losing one's balance.

It should be noted that the word we use in association with asana is 'practice' and not 'performance'. Falling is a very natural and humbling part of the journey. So, in this, and in all balance postures really, keeping one's sense of humour is arguably just as important as keeping the balance itself!

6

Padma-asana
The Lotus Pose

Padma means a lotus. Draw a square on a piece of paper. Now draw another square over the first, rotating it at a 45-degree angle. You will get an eight-pointed star. In Tantra, this represents the eight-petalled lotus, the womb of all existence. It also represents our mind, waiting to bloom through the practice of yoga. The realization of potential through the practice of yoga is symbolically visualized as the sequential blooming of lotus flowers along the spinal cord, each flower having more petals than the one before it with the final one in the head having a thousand petals.

Eight-petalled lotus

The lotus blooms in muck but remains unblemished, thus representing purity and rising above the dirt that is

59

the material world. The water rolling off its petals suggests detachment. The gradual unfurling of its petals to reveal its nectar that attracts bees represents fertility. Thus, the lotus embodies paradoxical ideas: detachment, as well as the pleasures of life.

Padma

It is said that when the world began it bloomed in the presence of consciousness like the lotus flowers in the sun. Thus, the lotus is considered a symbol of creation. Brahma, the creator, sits on a lotus flower that rises from Vishnu's navel. Vishnu, the preserver, is also shown holding a lotus flower. Lakshmi, the goddess of wealth, is also associated with the lotus. The lotuses in her hand attract bees and butterflies towards her.

In Hindu art, a woman depicted holding a lotus bud is deemed a virgin; when she holds a lotus in bloom, she is regarded as mature and experienced. Images of a goddess who exposes her genitals, carries lotuses in her hands, and whose head is made of a lotus flower, have been found across India. She is nameless though some people call her Lajjagauri, the shy mother goddess. She is said

Lajjagauri

to be Shakti, who covered her face out of modesty when sages trespassed into the forest where she was making love to Shiva.

In Thervada Buddhism, it is believed that when Buddha emerged from his mother's womb, he was able to walk, and wherever he stepped a lotus bloomed. In the Pure Land, or Sukhavati, described in Mahayana Buddhism, every Buddha is born not from a woman's womb but from a lotus flower. The Buddhist goddess Tara, born of Buddha's tears of compassion for the suffering world, is often shown holding a lotus flower in her hand. She is linked with knowledge.

One of the forms of Buddha is called Padmapani – he who holds the lotus in his hand. Once, a young man, seeking to understand the meaning of the long discourse given by Buddha on Buddhism, asked Buddha if he could explain the discourse using a gesture or a symbol. Buddha simply picked up a lotus flower. At that moment, just looking at the lotus flower, the young man understood the meaning of Buddhism. That is when the famous mantra came into being: 'Om mani padme hum', the jewel which is locked within the lotus flower. This is a metaphor which means many things. The jewel can be knowledge that pollinates the mind-lotus. The jewel can represent the man's seed and the lotus flower can represent the woman's womb. The jewel can also symbolize consciousness and the lotus flower, the material world. The jewel can also be the Buddha rising from the lotus flower, a common representation in Mahayana Buddhist art.

Padmapani Bodhisattva

Birth of Buddha from a lotus

In Jain mythology, Padma is the name of Ram in the Ramayana. Unlike the Hindu Ramayana, the Jain Ramayana sees Padma as non-violent, leaving the killing of Ravana to his younger brother, Lakshman. In Jain lore, we also learn of a queen who loved a couch covered with lotus flowers. Her son was named Padmaprabha, he with the glow of a lotus. The son grew up to be the sixth of twenty-four Jinas, symbolized by a lotus flower.

With good reason, Padma-asana may be the most widely recognized asana, and probably the most frequently associated with the practice of yoga and meditation. It offers the most stable seated position available to the human form by providing maximum contact between the legs and the ground. It also allows for the ideal bodily posture and spinal alignment associated with pranayama (breath control practices) that are often done in conjunction with asanas. In Sanskrit, padma is a reference to a lotus plant, and the lotus itself can only thrive in the stillness of calm water.

7

Baka-asana
The Crane Pose

Baka refers to a crane. In Hindu mythology, the crane is associated with concentration, one who waits patiently with deep focus and, in so doing, is able to catch fish from the water. Therefore, the crane is, sometimes, associated with the goddess of knowledge, Saraswati.

In the Mahabharata, a yaksha, in the form of a crane, is the guardian of a lake, and does not allow anyone to drink water from it unless they answer his questions. Those who drink without answering die instantly. Four of the five Pandava brothers, in royal arrogance, refuse to answer the questions; they drink the water and perish. The eldest brother, Yudhisthira, however, defers to the wishes of the crane and answers his

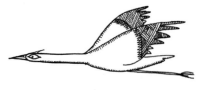

Baka

questions. One of the questions the crane asks is: What is the greatest wonder in the world? Yudhisthira replies that the greatest wonder in the world is that people die every day, but the living live life as if they are immortal. Pleased with Yudhisthira's answers, the

Yudhisthira and the crane

crane restores life to all his brothers.

Krishna killing Baka, the demon

The Baka is also referred to as a demon occasionally. In the Bhagavata Purana that retells the story of Krishna's childhood, a gigantic crane attacks Krishna and his friend when they are grazing their cows in a pasture along the riverbank. Krishna kills the giant crane by tearing its beak apart.

The Baka is sometimes linked to the goddess Saraswati, goddess of knowledge, and is considered the symbol of patience and concentration, waiting till it finds a fish and then darting forth to grab it.

Herons and cranes often stand on one foot, to fool fish into believing their solitary legs are reeds. When a fish comes near a heron's leg, it immediately catches hold of its hapless prey. Standing on one foot is also a yoga posture. Therefore, the elongated straight leg of the yogi has led

Bagula Bhagat

Yoga Mythology: 64 Asanas and their Stories

the charlatan yogi to be called 'bagula bhagat', a modern Hindi term for a crook who pretends to be a hermit – for, like the crane who stands on one foot, his main intention is to catch the proverbial fish.

Often confused with the bent-arm posture Kakka-asana, this pose represents a long-legged water bird and is practised with the arms locked straight. It requires a great deal of upper body and core strength to maintain, and is considerably less dependent on bone support than its bent-arm counterpart. In practice, the best description of this posture boils down to leaning the hips and shoulders far enough forward to balance while pressing into the fingertips just hard enough so as not to fall on one's face. Another important aspect of this pose is how the head is oriented. Out of fear of falling, it is often very tempting to keep the head turned down and the eyes fixed on the ground when getting into this pose, but keeping the head lifted and the eyes forward helps the practitioner maintain bodily awareness with respect to the horizon (even if you're practicing indoors). Mastering balance in Kakka-asana can be a good metric for determining when one is ready to progress to Baka-asana, the more advanced arm-balance posture.

8

Krauncha-asana
The Heron Pose

The difference between a baka (crane) and a krauncha (heron) is that the former's neck is elongated straight, while the latter's neck is curved when they are flying.

In a folk Ramayana, when Ram returns from a deer hunt and finds his wife, Sita, absent from their house, he wonders where she is. A heron tells Ram that it knows her whereabouts but will not tell him. Angrily, Ram catches hold of its neck and bends it, which is why the heron has a bent neck. Later, the heron apologizes and reveals that Sita has been abducted by the demon-king Ravana. As she was being taken away Sita's tears fell on the ground, and one teardrop fell on to the heron's body, which is why it now has white feathers.

Krauncha

In another story from the Ramayana, a pair of krauncha birds are circling each other in love play. A hunter strikes the male heron dead. The poet Valmiki sees the female heron wailing piteously over her mate's body. Moved by this tragic sight, Valmiki curses the hunter, the words slipping out of his mouth in the form of poetry. Pain, thus, gives rise to poetry, incidentally the first poem in the world, which is why Valmiki is called the first poet of the world. He composed the epic

Krauncha mourning
the killing of its mate

Ramayana in lyric form after this event. The story of the krauncha birds and the longing of one for its mate, forms a recurring theme in the epic, where lovers are separated by circumstances and war, making Valmiki's Ramayana not so much a heroic epic as a romantic epic. It must be appreciated not just as a great tale of war but as a tale of human longing and suffering caused by the absence of a beloved.

In the southern part of India, there is Krauncha Mountain or Heron Mountain which is characterized by a split in its middle, creating a pass. Some say the passage makes the mountain range look like the heron's bent neck. Others say the split in the mountain was created by a spear hurled by the war-god Kartikeya at a demon who hid in this mountain in the form of a heron.

Krauncha is also a proper noun. It refers to a man who accidentally stepped on a sage's foot, and was turned into a rat. This rat caused so much havoc in the world that the gods begged the elephant-headed Ganesha to intervene. Ganesha immediately caught Krauncha, the rat, and made him his vehicle (vahana) so he could not cause any more trouble.

The heron is the symbol of Sumati-nath, the fifth Jina of this eon.

Jina Sumati-nath

This elegant seated posture involves an internal rotation of the bent hip and a deep hamstring stretch in the straight leg. Perhaps a reference to the long legs of an aquatic bird, or a subtle reference to the arrow that struck Valmiki's heron in the stream. This asana can be considered an advanced progression of Tiriang Mukhaikapada Paschimottana-asana (oblique one-leg back stretching pose), a popular asana in the Iyengar and Ashtanga yoga traditions, which essentially has the same orientation of the limbs, except the body is folded forward over the front leg instead of the leg being raised to meet the body. The slight curvature of the spine could also be a reference to the bent neck of the heron.

9

Kakka-asana
The Crow Pose

The crow is frequently placed in contrast to the crane, possibly because the former is often seen on garbage dumps, while the latter is associated with water. The crane is white in colour and associated with knowledge, while the crow, with its black colour, is associated with death and things that are inauspicious. The crow has shorter limbs and is a land bird, unlike the crane which has long limbs and is a water bird. They, in a way, represent a contrast between the fixed and the fluid states of life.

In the Ramayana, Jayanta, son of Indra, king of the devas, took the form of a crow and disturbed Ram and Sita while they were in the forest. Annoyed by the crow incessantly chasing Sita, Ram took a blade of grass and pierced one of the bird's eyes. This is why it is believed that a crow can only see from one side at a time and moves its head this way or that. In reality,

Kakabhushundi, the wise crow

both eyes of a crow are functional but it chooses to see with one eye at a time as its monocular vision is better than binocular vision.

In the Bhagavata Purana, a demon takes the form of a crow and attacks Krishna when he is still a baby. But Krishna catches hold of the crow's feet and slays it, quite like Hercules despatches the snake that tries to kill him. There are many stories of Krishna that have parallels with those of Hercules, leading scholars to speculate that these stories emerged when the Greeks entered India, after Alexander's great march eastward.

Kakabhushundi is an immortal crow, who overhears a conversation between Shiva and Shakti, and conveys it to the rest of the world. He knows things that no one else does, as he has travelled around the world, having been granted immortality. Kakabhushundi is often associated with sages and storytellers. The crow is thus associated with wisdom. It is also associated with death. In Hindu funeral ceremonies, rice balls are

Krishna capturing the demon crow

offered to crows and, if the crows eat them, it means that the ancestors are happy.

Crows are also linked with the planet Shani, or Saturn, who, according to Hindu mythology, delays things, forcing humans to be patient. The cawing of the crow, depending on the time, can be considered auspicious or inauspicious. Auspiciously, it indicates the arrival of guests; inauspiciously, it indicates the arrival of a ghost.

Crow, a symbol of ancestors

This asana is usually the first exposure to arm balances that most practitioners experience and is arguably the easiest to find balance in. With the upper arm parallel to the floor, the knees have a reliable support structure on which to rest. As previously mentioned and in keeping with a fundamental principle of almost all arm-balance postures, keeping the shoulders in a position that is forward of the wrists is necessary to maintain even distribution of the body's weight over the base of support. The bent arms also help keep the body's centre of mass (the hips) lower to the ground which in turn gives a little more control over the balance, since less effort is required to shift the hips forward or backwards.

10

Kukkuta-asana
The Rooster Pose

The rooster embodies the alpha male. It is known for the pecking order it creates in its harem. On account of its virility and aggressive nature, it is associated with the planet Mangal, or Mars, and with the god of war, known as Murugan in south India and as Kartikeya in north India. Kartikeya is the son of Shiva and Shakti and the commander of the celestial armies, who defeated the asura Taraka. On his banner is displayed the rooster, indicating his virile status.

A folk Ramayana describes how when Ram returns from a deer hunt and discovers Sita missing, he fears that she has left him, having tired of the hardships in the forest. At that point a rooster informs Ram that it is not so and

Kukkuta

that Sita has been abducted by Ravana. Relieved that his wife has not abandoned him, the grateful Ram gifts the rooster a golden crown. But the rooster begs Ram to change this gift, as people were already chasing after him for his meat, and now he feared they would run after him for his golden crown. Therefore, Ram, with compassion, turns the golden crown into a crown of skin, red in colour, on the rooster's head.

The Hijras of India, who identify themselves as the third gender, neither male nor female, worship Bahuchara-mata, a goddess who rides a rooster. The story goes that a princess discovered that her husband, who never came to her bedchambers, preferred to ride out into the woods at night. She could not follow him as she had no horse, but a giant rooster offered to help her chase her husband. In the forest, the princess discovered her husband dressed in women's clothes and engaged in homosexual activities. Furious that

Bahuchara-mata

he had kept his true desires secret and had tricked her into marriage, she castrated him and transformed into a goddess, who rides a rooster. The goddess appears in dreams of men with desires similar to her husband's, and gives them the strength to admit the truth of their gender and sexuality and to withstand social pressures that force them to enter heterosexual relationships. Society may marginalize the queer, from cross-dressers, eunuchs, transgender people to homosexuals, but not this goddess who rides the rooster.

In the Buddhist wheel of life, the rooster represents our attachments, and is often depicted along with the pig (symbolic of attraction) and snake (symbolic of revulsion). Together they are the indicators of craving that make life unhappy.

Buddhist symbols of craving

A complex arm balance, this posture requires the legs to be folded into a full lotus (Padma-asana) position. The arms are then extended through the folded legs between the calves and the backs of the thighs for each arm respectively. Balance in this posture is maintained by keeping the shoulders slightly forward of the wrists, a technique which is fundamentally true for almost all arm-balance postures. The resultant form, with the fingers spread wide, looks very much like the legs of a rooster, giving rise to the name.

11

Gomukha-asana
The Cow-face Pose

G omukha means a cow's face. The cow is sacred in
Hinduism; in ancient times, it was one of the few
animals from which food could be obtained without hurting
the animal. It not only provided food; it also provided fuel
in the form of dung. This made it a very auspicious animal.
In later times, cows became a metaphor for a sustainable
livelihood, as well as for the earth.

Cows are closely associated with
Krishna, also known as Gopala, the
cowherd, and are also a metaphor for
the earth, the vegetation of the earth
representing their milk. The earth goddess
is often visualized as a cow in the Puranas
and the kings of the earth are described as
her caretakers.

Gomukha

The river Ganga is said to have originated from the mouth of a cow and hence the traditional origin of the river is from a place called Gomukh. The pouch in which devotees keep their sacred string of memory beads represents a cow's mouth and therefore is also called Gomukh.

In architecture, a narrow opening that leads to a wider space is called Gomukh. A cow's mouth is narrower than her forehead. This trapezoid shape, with the outer part narrow and the inner part wide, is traditionally associated with the Gomukh. Its opposite is the Singhamukh which is the lion's face, also trapezoid but with the wider end in front and the narrow end behind – used especially in Hindu temples, where entrances are large and inviting but the actual deity is located in a tiny dark chamber inside, lit by oil and ghee lamps. Traditional Indian houses follow the Gomukh architecture, so they look very small from the outside, but one realizes their scale only when one enters the main courtyard beyond the narrow passage. One practical reason for this is to ensure invaders cannot enter the city or settlement easily. Ancient Egyptian temples also follow the Gomukh style and that has led to speculation that there was some connection between ancient India and ancient Egypt. However, temples in ancient Egypt are over 3000 years old while temples in India are just over 1000 years old. So the similarity may be a coincidence. But we cannot be sure.

Gomukha yaksha

In many temple traditions, the rear of the cow is considered more auspicious than the head because from the rear end, one can clearly see the udders that give milk and the anal opening from which one gets dung which can be used as fuel and fertilizer, as well as natural insect repellent material for layering the floor and the walls of a traditional hut.

In Jain temples, the images of the Tirthankaras, also known as Jinas, are flanked by images of a yaksha and a yakshi. These were ancient local gods who were made part of the Jain pantheon. The cow-faced yaksha, Gomukha, is the guardian of Rishabha, the first of the twenty-four Jinas of this eon.

Go means 'cow' in Sanskrit, and mukha means 'face'. Resembling the face of a cow, this pose involves a tight crossing of the legs and cross-binding of the hands at the back. Known for considerably intense stretching of the shoulders, this pose is often worked up to by initially connecting the hands with a belt or strap. In my experience, it has always been easiest to make the hand connection by starting with the lower arm, then raising the top arm over to meet it, and this same process can be incorporated when using a strap as well. The leg positioning can be especially challenging for men or for practitioners with knee injuries, so padding with a blanket or modifying the position of the legs is often helpful and encouraged.

———————

12

Vrischika-asana
The Scorpion Pose

Once upon a time, there was a sage who was bathing in a river. When he stepped on the riverbank, he found a scorpion trapped between two rocks, desperately struggling to escape. The sage freed the scorpion by moving the rocks. As soon as it was free, the scorpion stung the sage with its poisonous tail before scampering away. An onlooker laughed and told the sage that it served him right to save a scorpion. To which the sage replied, 'I behaved as per my nature and it behaved as per its own.' We must each live our lives as per our nature, without being influenced by other people. The story draws on a very important yogic philosophy – swabhav or our inner personality.

Vrischika

Do we live our lives true to our nature or do we constantly adapt or pretend to adapt to the environment around us that knots our minds, knots that can only be removed through yogic practices?

The scorpion, in Hindu mythology, is associated with the goddess Chamunda, who is also known as the scorpion-bellied goddess. In art, she is depicted as a gaunt, emaciated goddess with many arms, who is associated with crematoriums and battlefields. She is surrounded by corpses and ghosts and feeds on the entrails of the dead. Her concave stomach

Chamunda

displays a scorpion which adds to her ferocity. She is a frightening goddess. This image, in a non-Hindu set-up, may be seen as that of a demoness or a witch, but in Hindu mythology, gods and goddesses take various forms, some romantic, some lovable, some delightful and some frightening, so that all human emotions are expressed through them. Thus, for Hindus, this is the form of the goddess. Even the crematorium, ghosts and goblins are part of the divine scheme of things.

In Tantric traditions, it is by meditating on these inauspicious, frightening and undesirable things that we can see the true nature of the world and attain wisdom.

In the famous temple sculptures of Khajuraho, one finds beautiful women disrobing themselves on the excuse that a scorpion is climbing up their thighs. This is a metaphor for extreme sexual excitement at the sight of a scorpion, which clearly is a symbol for the male sexual organ or the predatory male instinct. Here, there is an open acknowledgment of aggressive and even toxic masculine behaviour, which is not feared but gently domesticated by the damsels, who are identified as yoginis.

Scared temple maiden

This posture resembles the curled tail of a scorpion ready to strike its prey and incorporates the challenge of a back bend into an already tricky inverted position. A common problem that students face when first practicing this posture is the floor, and by that, I mean that they go up into the inversion but find their face is almost touching the floor. This is caused by an initial fear response which compels the practitioner to bring their shoulders as far forward as possible when, in fact, the ideal position for the shoulders is directly stacked above the elbows. This orientation offers the most ground clearance for the head, and by stacking the upper arm bones vertically, the balance is then reliant on bone support instead of pure muscular exertion.

———————————

13

Manjara-asana
The Cat Pose

The cat, whether wild or domestic, is associated with the mother goddess. One sees the goddesses Durga and Kali riding lions and tigers as they rush into battle. The cat's feline, secretive nature has long been associated with witchcraft; but traditionally, in Hindu lore, it is associated with a goddess. The king's throne is called the simhasana, the lion throne, and the cat was considered to be the guardian of kings, especially because of its fierce and independent spirit. During festivals of the goddess, in many parts of south India, the tiger dance is performed by men. The tiger is also the form taken by Bhuta, local guardian deities of Tulu-nadu, in the southern state of Karnataka.

The domestic cat, specifically, is associated with the goddess Sashthi or Satwai, who facilitates childbirth. Perhaps this association is linked to how the cat takes care of its kittens by

Sashthi's manjara

catching them by the scruff of their necks and carrying them to safe places, away from the murderous claws of the tomcat. As an embodiment of the maternal instinct, she protects as well as nurtures.

In the southern state of Kerala there is a story of the prince Manikantha who was asked by his stepmother to fetch the milk of the tigress to cure her of an ailment. He returned with a streak of tigresses, revealing he was no ordinary child but a divine being. Realizing that his stepmother had planned this ruse in order to secure the throne for his own son, Manikantha renounced the throne, made his half-brother king, and took refuge atop a mountain as a yogi. Many Hindus

Ayyappa Manikantha

see him as a child of Shiva and Vishnu, when the latter took the female form of Mohini. This queer birth has earned him the title of Hariharan, the child of Vishnu-Hari, god who gives wisdom, and Shiva-Hara, god who takes ignorance.

In the Buddhist Jatakas, the cat is often shown as a cunning villain, tricking roosters (by proposing marriage) and rats (by pretending to be an ascetic), with the intention of eating them.

In Vajrayana Buddhism, the great teacher Padmasambhava, often called the Second Buddha, is visualized riding a tigress. This tigress is his spiritual consort, the mother of Vajrayana Buddhism, a princess who transformed herself into a cat to enable Padmasambhava to travel to the most distant peaks of the Himalayas, where he could defeat demons and help people appreciate the wisdom of the Buddhist way.

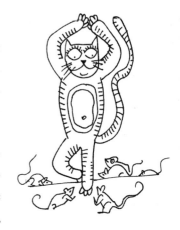

Cat, the pseudo-sage

Offering a gentle flexion of the spine, the Manjara-asana is commonly used as a warm-up posture in preparation for more rigorous forms of asana practice. It is often done dynamically along with the Gomukha-asana (with a convex curve to the spine) as part of a spinal warming sequence. This asana is usually entered from a neutral spine, or 'table-top' position, and is done on the exhale of the breath cycle. Simple modifications to make this posture more accessible might include placing padding under the knees and ankles or placing blocks under the hands to limit the overall worked range of motion.

14

Makara-asana
The Crocodile Pose

Makara is the Indian equivalent of Capricorn. While in Western mythology, Capricorn has a goat's head and a fish's tail, in Hindu mythology, it has an elephant's head and a fish's tail. It is sometimes associated with the fresh river dolphin from the Ganges. This zodiac sign marks the transformation of winter to spring and is an emblem of the love god, Kamadeva. Krishna, also symbolic of love, wears makara-shaped earrings. The makara is also the vehicle of the river goddess Ganga, and of the sea god Varuna. It is the symbol of fertility, life, spring and joy.

Ganga on makara

The makara is often confused with magara, the crocodile, due to

Magara

their similar sounding names. The crocodile is a metaphor for worldly attachments that entrap us. While the makara refers to the bounty of material life, the magara is a warning of the perils of materialism.

Once, the elephant-king Gajendra was bathing in a lotus pond, and enjoying the company of his queens, when suddenly his foot was snared by a crocodile intent on drowning him. Gajendra's wives ran away and no one came to his rescue, until he picked up a lotus flower and offered it to any god who heard his plea. Then Vishnu appeared from the sky on his eagle, Garuda, hurled his discus and struck down the crocodile, liberating Gajendra.

Makara

Crocodile trapping the elephant

In the Ramayana, we hear of how an apsara who disturbed a yogi was cursed and turned into a crocodile until she was overpowered by Hanuman. A similar story is told in the Mahabharata, where five apsaras were turned into crocodiles when they tried to enchant a yogi; they were overpowered and liberated by Arjuna. These stories equate the crocodile's grip to that of the power of lust.

In Buddhist art, the makara is the symbol of tenacity and is a popular motif in Sri Lankan Theravada Buddhism as well as Tibetan Vajrayana Buddhism. It is found as a decorative motif across the Buddhist world, from Japan to Thailand.

Jina Pushpadanta

The Jatakas tell the story of a crocodile who offered to help a monkey cross the river on his back. But the monkey who was the Buddha-to-be soon realized the crocodile intended to drown him midway and eat his heart, which he believed was tasty as the monkey ate berries all day. The monkey convinced the crocodile into taking him back to the shore, saying, 'I have left my heart on the berry tree.'

The makara is the symbol of Pushpadanta, the ninth Jina of this eon.

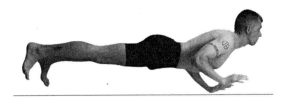

Another dynamic asana, this posture represents the chomping of a crocodile's jaws. From the plank position known as Chaturanga Danda-asana in yoga, quickly and powerfully pressing into the hands to 'jump' off the floor while strongly engaging the musculature of the back allows the lower body to remain in-line with the upper body. In practice, this posture is usually done by jumping forward a set number of repetitions followed by jumping back the same number of repetitions to return to the starting position. Another variation of this asana by the same name offers a much less strenuous form and is often considered much more accessible to novice practitioners. In this variation, the front of body is usually laid flat against the ground with the head supported by the hands and elbows in a relatively relaxed manner.

***

15

Bhujanga-asana
The Cobra Pose

Although there are many varieties of snakes in India, it is the cobra that has great significance in Indic mythology, particularly in yoga. The cobra is considered special because of its hood, which it raises whenever confronted with danger. When the hood flares up, it indicates the cobra is still, alert, ready to strike. Therefore, the hooded cobra indicates a moment of stillness, as opposed to the coiled cobra which indicates restraint, potential energy waiting to be unleashed. The copulating serpent indicates movement. These three depictions are found across temples in India.

In Jainism, Buddhism and Hinduism, it is believed that below the earth is Naga-loka, the realm of snakes. These are not ordinary

Bhujanga

serpents; they are shape-shifting beings with gems on their hoods known as naga-mani, jewels that are believed to contain magical, curative properties. In popular lore, the snakes come to the earthly realms in human form, and have relationships with human beings.

The serpent coiled around Shiva's neck is Karkotaka. Some identify this serpent as Patanjali, who overheard the conversation of yoga between Shiva and Shakti, which led him to write the Yoga-sutra. In popular art, Patanjali is visualized as a serpent. He is shown holding a conch-shell trumpet and a wheel, symbols of breath and the cyclical nature of the world, which link him to Vishnu.

While a cobra coils itself around Shiva's neck, Vishnu lies on the coils of one (Adisesha), and as Krishna he dances on another's hood (Kaliya). In many literatures, the whole world rests on Adisesha's hood. Vishnu himself sleeps on Adisesha's coils, with his hood serving as a kind of parasol. Adisesha

Jina Parsva-nath

is special as he has multiple heads. In Jainism, such a multi-headed serpent forms the parasol for the Jina Parsva-nath. When Buddha became the awakened one, another multi-hooded serpent rose to protect him from rain and sun. We can see how the coiled hooded serpent came to be associated with the still wisdom of Indian sages. A similar serpent sheltered the infant Krishna from the rains when he was being taken across the river Yamuna

Yoga Mythology: 64 Asanas and their Stories

by his father, Vasudev, who was determined to protect his son from the murderous Kansa, king of Mathura.

The king of the serpents is called Vasuki and his sister is called Manasa. Manasa is worshipped in many parts of India to protect people from snakebite.

Unlike Christian mythology, where the serpent of Eden is considered evil, in Hindu mythology, the serpent is considered an auspicious symbol. Serpents are worshipped across India to ensure the fertility of land, as well as for children. They are associated with mystical as well as occult powers. In yoga, the famous Kundalini Shakti or coiled energy rises up the spine in the form of copulating serpents, uniting in the head, in the famous chakra system.

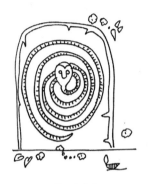

Kundalini

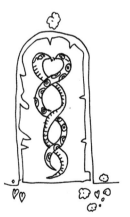

Serpent shrine

In Jain mythology, time is imagined as moving like a serpent, curving up towards good times and curving down towards bad times. Each curve of time is an eon that witnesses the arrival of sixty-three great beings: twenty-four Jinas, twelve Chakravartis and nine pacifist Baladevas, whose brothers, the Vasudevas, are violent heroes who defeat their enemy, the Prati-vasudevas. The Vasudevas seeks to control the world, Chakravartis organize the world and Jinas understand the world.

In Sanskrit, bhujanga means 'snake' or 'serpent'. Taking the shape of a snake poised to strike, this posture is often used to introduce practitioners to the benefits of back-bending poses. Similar in appearance to the Upward-facing Dog pose, this pose is a little easier on the legs as they remain in contact with the floor, and the intensity of the bend in the back can be adjusted according to the degree of the bend in the arms. The gaze in this pose is traditionally upward but keeping the head neutral and looking straight ahead is an easy way to modify and relieve discomfort in the neck and shoulders.

16

Bheka-asana
The Frog Pose

In Vedic texts, children memorizing and repeating the rules of grammar are compared to croaking frogs.

According to a story from the Mahabharata, there was a frog princess who seduced young men, but when she got bored of them, she would request them to take her to a lake. There, she would go for a swim and never return – she would secretly transform back to her frog form and leave her human lover heartbroken. This happened several times. However, when she tried to abandon King Parikshit similarly, the king panicked and asked his soldiers to drain the entire pond. There they found a single bull frog who turned out to be the king of frogs and the father

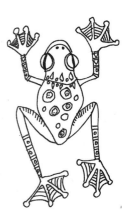

Bheka

Frog princess

of the princess. The king was about to kill this frog thinking that he had swallowed his princess when the princess reappeared, begged Parikshit for forgiveness and married him. One could say this is a local Indian version of 'The Frog Prince'.

In another story from the folk versions of the Ramayana, Ravana, the great king of Lanka, impressed Shiva so much with his songs that Shiva offered him a boon. Ravana said that he wanted to marry Shiva's wife Shakti. Shiva had no choice but to agree. But Shakti had a trick up her sleeve. She found a female frog, a manduka, and transformed her into a damsel, the very likeness of her. Ravana mistook her for Parvati and took her to Lanka but kept wondering why she only got excited in the rainy season on hearing the sounds of the bull frogs in the garden — for he never realized his wife was actually a frog.

According to the Jatakas, the Buddha was born as a frog in one of his previous lives. He saw a snake being attacked by a school of fish. The snake asked, 'Is this appropriate?' to which the frog replied, 'You eat the fish when they enter your territory. The fish attack you when you enter theirs. Considering the context, what is happening now is surely appropriate.'

Buddhists tell the story of how a frog who was reborn as a god after being trampled by a cowherd while listening to a sermon of the Buddha. The Jains tell the story of a merchant who was so attached to the idea of building a pond that he was reborn as a frog in that same pond. He overheard people praising him for building the pond but wondered why, despite this good deed, he was born as a frog. Then he heard the sermon of the Jina Mahavira and realized the folly of attachment. An elephant crushed him accidentally and he was reborn as a heavenly being on the path to liberation from the wheel of rebirth.

This back-bending asana offers a deep stretch across the fronts of the thighs as well as the chest and abdominals. Bheka is the Sanskrit word for 'frog' and the folding of the legs in this posture resembles the jumping legs of a frog. Practitioners usually approach this posture by coming into it from a modified Bhujanga-asana position (serpent pose), and it can be helpful to work one leg at a time before progressing into the full expression of the asana. As an intermediate back bend, this posture usually precedes the practicing of more complex, or 'deeper', back bends. Postures like Supta vira-asana (reclined hero pose), or its one-legged variation, provide a stretch for the legs in the same range of motion as Bheka-asana, and can be a good starting place for practitioners looking to explore this pose in particular.

17

Dhanura-asana
The Bow Pose

In Hindu mythology, the bow plays a very important role. Shiva's bow is known as Pinaka, Vishnu's is Saranga. Ram is the archer who never misses a target in the Ramayana; while Arjuna is the ace archer whose story is told in the Mahabharata. Yet, the bow is best associated with the Goddess, because she embodies nature, which functions on the principles of desire and hunger, thirst and yearning. The transformation of a non-living thing into a living organism involves the birth of desire, hunger, thirst and yearning. Hunger and thirst are hallmarks of living organisms. This is represented by the bow that is held in the hand of the Goddess. It is the bow of Kamadeva, the god of love, lust and desire.

Kamadeva's bow is made of sugarcane, the bowstring is made of bees and butterflies and the arrows are tipped

Dhanush

with flowers. With his arrows, Kamadeva fills the body with longing, much like Eros, the Greek god of love. When struck by Kama's five arrows, we come alive with desire; we yearn for food, satisfaction, pleasure and survival. In the hermit traditions of India, from Buddhism and Jainism to Hinduism, monks claim that desire is the cause of all suffering, and hunger is the cause of all pain. Therefore, the purpose of life should be to outgrow this hunger and desire. Thus Kamadeva becomes the enemy who must be destroyed, known in Buddhism as Mara, the demon of desire.

Shiva opens his third eye and sets aflame the god of love, reducing him to a heap of ash which he smears on his body. However, the Goddess confronts Shiva and demands that he resurrect Kamadeva because without kama, or love, nature cannot function. Why would a plant rise towards the sunlight if it has no desire? Why would the roots move towards water if they do not have thirst? Why would a tree produce flowers if it did not wish to reproduce? Why would animals graze? Why would they hunt? Why would human civilizations exist? Shiva realizes

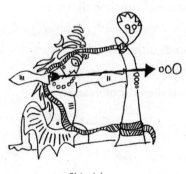

Shiva's bow

the dangers of curbing desire and the love god is resurrected in the form of the goddess Kamakshi or Kamini, one who evokes desire. She carries Kamadeva's bow to remind the hermits that desire matters, nature matters, all conversations of transcendence notwithstanding.

Yoga Mythology: 64 Asanas and their Stories

The bow is sometimes considered the symbol of yoga, with which desires are brought under control. The body is the bow, the breath the bowstring, and awareness is the arrow with which the yoga practitioner connects with the truth of life, the world, nature and culture. Shiva uses his bow to pin Brahma to the sky when the creator,

Kama's bow

overcome by lust, pursues the Goddess, intent on controlling her. Shiva also used Mount Meru, the axis of space, as the shaft of his bow, and the serpent of time, Adisesha, as the string of his bow to let loose the single arrow – Vishnu himself – that destroyed three flying cities of asuras, worlds that had gone decadent. That is why Shiva smears his body with three horizontal lines of ash.

Commonly serving as a progression of back-bending postures, this asana is aptly named for its resemblance to a bow and its string. The arching legs and torso represent the shaft of the bow itself and the straight arms represent a bow string pulled taut. While many variations of this asana are often practised, this particular version is one of the few postures that actively engages the 'pulling' musculature of the back. Gentler variations of this posture involve separating the feet and knees, or using a belt or strap to complete the connection between the ankles and the hands.

18

Pasha-asana
The Noose Pose

In Hindu mythology, nature is governed by two principles: desire and destiny. Desire propels action, action results in a reaction and reaction creates the circumstances we experience and from which we cannot escape. In other words, desire eventually creates destiny. If desire is represented by the bow, then destiny is represented by the pasha, or noose, that binds us to experience the destiny created by our own desires. This is karma.

People often confuse karma with fatalism. However, that is an incomplete understanding of karma. Karma is both action and reaction. Action includes both voluntary actions and involuntary action. Reactions manifest as the circumstances that we experience. All that happens to us in life is karma; how we react or respond to the events of our life is also karma.

Pasha

Pasha is visualized as a lasso or a knot: it is the noose of Yama, the god of death and rebirth. He maintains the record of all our actions: the debts we incur in our life, through desire, which we must repay in a future life. Only when we repay all our debts will the noose liberate us and we will attain what is called moksha or mukti: freedom from hunger, fear, attachment and the circle of life and death.

The Goddess embodies nature. She carries the twin qualities of both desire and destiny, therefore she is often known as both Kamini and Yamini. As Kamini, she carries the sugarcane bow with the flower-tipped arrows of Kama. As Yamini, she carries the noose of Yama that binds us to our destiny. As Kamini, she is the day. As Yamini, she is the night. She completes the world.

One must bear in mind that the concept of God as a judge, which is part of Christian and Islamic mythology, is absent in Hindu mythology. In Christian mythology, we live only once and at the end of our life we are judged based on our actions. Hindu mythology speaks of rebirth, a cycle wherein God does not play the role of a judge. We pay for our actions through the reactions that are created by our actions. These reactions create either good or bad circumstances of our life, which we are obliged to endure in our future lives. When it is our time to die, Yama hurls the noose and pulls the life-breath out of our bodies. He keeps us tied to this noose until we've repaid our debts, which are essentially the reactions of past actions. So, we can say, that at one level, Yama's noose embodies the fate that is in store for us, while Kama's bow and arrow hold a potential of actions that we choose in response to the destiny we encounter. But just as past desires through actions establish current destiny, current desires through actions establish future destiny. Thus, we shape our past as well as our future. We cannot blame anyone; we alone are responsible for our lives. This is the complete explanation of karma in Hindu mythology.

As theism became popular in India, especially over the last 1000 years, the belief that appealing to Shiva and Vishnu enables us to escape the noose of Yama became popular. And so emerged stories of how Shiva rescues his devotee, Markandeya, who was chanting his name, from Yama at the moment of death. Vishnu rescues a scoundrel called Ajamila from Yama's noose simply because he called out to his son named Vishnu.

Devotional movements offered a way out from the fetters of destiny, as an alternative to the ascetic solutions offered by monastic orders such as Buddhism and Jainism. Freedom using the devotional route was bhakti yoga, while freedom using meditation was gyan yoga, and freedom from detached performance of one's destined role, without desiring results, was karma yoga.

Yama's noose

Representing the knot of a noose, this posture requires a great deal of spinal rotation and shoulder mobility to get a full binding of the hands. Revolved poses like this one employ a technique known as Uddhiyana Bandha (loosely translated as 'abdominal lock') which involves the drawing in and lifting up of the lower abdomen. This action provides the space needed for the rotation, but also kneads the lower abdominal organs, aiding in digestion and improving gastro-intestinal health. In addition to a deep bodily twist, this posture also requires a considerable amount of practice to stay upright and balanced, especially if it is difficult to get the heels down to the ground. A simple modification like placing a rolled blanket, or even a rolled yoga mat, under the heels can help provide an increased sense of stability while working towards a deeper spinal rotation, in turn making the posture more accessible to practitioners with limited flexibility or limited range of motion in the lower legs.

Brahma

Brahma is the creator god in Hinduism. However, Brahma is not worshipped. This is incomprehensible to many people, because the assumption is that he who creates the world must be worthy of worship. In fact, this idea that the creator should be worshipped comes to us from Judeo-Christian-Islamic (Abrahamic) mythology. But when we talk about Brahma and his creation, the reference is not to the creation of nature; he creates culture.

The act of creation begins with Brahma's awareness of himself, his hunger, the world around him, his fear of the unknown and his yearning for companionship, which leads him to domesticate

Brahma

nature, control fire and water, plants and animals, establish households, farms and markets. This process is facilitated by his mind-born sons, known as rishis or sages. These are no ordinary sages, but people who have observed the world and understood how it functions. The rishis communicated the wisdom of the universe through special chants known as mantras that are documented in Vedic literature.

Traditionally, Brahma is visualized as a priest, performing the fire ritual of exchange known as yagna, which creates culture. He is visualized as having four heads – these symbolize the four directions which he saw when he first created life. From the four heads, he gave rise to the four Vedas: Rig, which contains hymns; Sama, which contains melodies; Yajur, which contains rituals; and Atharva, which contains doctrine and spells for daily life. They also represent the four shastras: Dharma-shastra, which deals with governance; Artha-shastra, which deals with economics and politics; Kama-shastra, which deals with pleasure and art; and Moksha-shastra, which deals with wisdom that liberates us from hunger and fear, and therefore the cycle of birth and death.

Brahma's creation may be classified into two groups: the mind-born sons or the rishis, and his grandchildren who are born of the mind-born sons and have material bodies that experience death. Unlike the rishis who have the wisdom of the universe, the grandchildren struggle for life, and seek meaning. The rishis therefore codified yoga to help Brahma's grandchildren discover their true potential, to find peace beyond hunger and fear.

Among Brahma's grandchildren are the devas and the asuras as well. The devas live above earth, in the sky, in swarg or paradise, and have everything, while the asuras live below the earth and covet everything that the devas have. The devas have prosperity but no peace as they are constantly attacked by the asuras. This theme of brothers, half-brothers and cousins fighting over what they consider their fair share of the world is a consistent theme in Hindu mythology. It reveals how we define our value by our possessions and so continually fight for a greater share, greater value. But this value is imaginary and temporary, a delusion (maya).

Brahma is sometimes described as having the goddess of knowledge, Saraswati, as his consort. However, in stories, he is shown to chase the Goddess and she keeps running away to evade him. In early literature, it is Brahma's pursuit of the Goddess that gives rise to all living creatures, male and female. He is thus someone who is pursuing, who is seeking, and is not enlightened. He fails to recognize the truth of nature – she is his mother and daughter, and so his pursuit is condemned as 'incest'. The enlightened form of God is that of Shiva and Vishnu: Shiva who outgrows hunger and fear and Vishnu who pays attention to the hunger and fear of others. Thus Brahma, Vishnu, and Shiva embody the psychological response of living creatures through the

Saraswati, knowledge and the arts

material universe. The Hindu view of God has more to do with the evolution of the mind, and less to do with rules.

All humans are essentially Brahma, because of all living creatures they are the only ones with the ability to outgrow their instinct, their animal nature and reflect on the nature of society. This is why only humans have the potential to transform into rishis, discover the truth of the universe and outgrow hunger and fear to become like Shiva and Vishnu. In art, Hindu gods are given human form to acknowledge the divine potential of humanity, but the gods always have multiple heads or arms, to establish their higher state of consciousness, an expanded mind which understands how the world functions, and is not trapped by hunger and fear.

Brahma's name is closely linked to the idea of Brahman and Brahmin. Brahman is a Vedic concept that refers to the expansion (brah in Sanskrit) of the mind (manas). Our minds are contracted. Yoga helps us expand them to the infinite and realize the true nature of the limitless, timeless word. We outgrow all hunger and fear and are filled with tranquillity and love. This state of Brahman is what Hindus associate with God. In stories, this state becomes an entity such as Shiva and Vishnu. Brahma and his children embody the journey to Brahman. There are many ways of realizing Brahman, of which yoga is one. These techniques are communicated in Vedic literature, whose custodians were the Brahmins. We can say that Brahmins were given the responsibility to transmit Vedic literature that enables the Brahma within us to realize Brahman.

19

Omkar-asana
The Primal Sound Pose

Omkar means the form, or akar, of the primal sound, Om. Hindu chants typically begin with the syllable 'Om'. It is the primal sound of the universe: the first sound that created the series of vibrations that eventually lead to the creation of life. Some believe it is inspired by the lowing of cows; ancient sages revered the cow as a symbol of the universe. It marks the birth of consciousness and therefore the birth of time, the past, present and future; the birth of space and its three axes; the birth of matter and its three states of being – inertia (tamas), agitation (rajas) and lucidity (sattva).

It's like the entrance to a house: to enter a house, you must cross the border. The syllable Om marks the 'entrance' to a chant. This practice is followed by Buddhists as well. In Buddhist shrines in Japan and China, one often finds a pair of guardians, one whose mouth is open and the other whose mouth is shut, marking the beginning and the end of the Om sound.

The idea of Om as sacred comes to us from the Upanishadic traditions and therefore, predates the Buddha, who lived about 2500 years ago. Om is the beej mantra or the seed, also known as the pranava, the seed sound from which all sounds emerge.

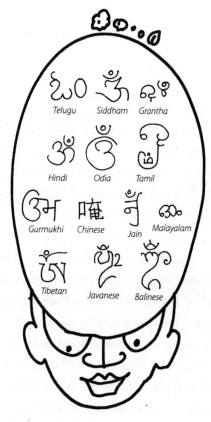

Om in different languages

In art, it is commonly associated with Ganesha, who is worshipped at the beginning of all rituals. Just as Om is chanted at the beginning of all hymns, Ganesha is worshipped at the start of all activities to remove obstacles. One can say therefore that Ganesha embodies the Om sound. This practice of transforming a magical sound into a deity is common in Hinduism. The Gayatri mantra, for example, is manifested as a goddess, just as Om is embodied as a god.

Jains see Om, or Aum, as an acronym for the five types of teachers: Arihant, Asharira, Acharya, Upajjhaya, Muni.

In Sikhism, 'Ek Omkar' is a phrase to refer to the single formless ultimate divine.

Om is the sacred vibration of creation, the primal or primordial sound. Sometimes spelled as Aum, it is comprised of the fundamental syllables: a-kara, u-kara and ma-kara. The word 'kara' also translates to 'action', and when combined with a syllable, it generally means to 'pronounce the sound of'. The asana's name is sometimes translated as 'Chanting of Om' pose, or 'Tribute to Om' pose. The body's shape in this arm-balance posture resembles the form of the symbol for Om, and elegant though it may appear, it is certainly one of the more challenging poses to work on. In the Ashtanga Vinyasa yoga tradition of Mysore, this posture is the very last in the fourth (of six) series of postures, and traditionally, one does not typically progress to a succeeding series until complete mastery of the preceding series is observed by one's acharya (teacher).

20

Hamsa-asana
The Swan Pose

While the word 'hamsa' is commonly used for a swan, many scholars believe it refers to the goose in Hindu mythology, and 'raj-hamsa' is used instead for the swan.

The hamsa is closely associated with the breathing practices found in yoga. The sound 'hum' involves exhalation and the sound 'so' involves inhalation and thus hamsa indicates expiration and inspiration. It is said that the swan/goose was created from the breath of Brahma.

The hamsa is the symbol of intellectual discernment because in folklore it is shown to have the ability to separate milk from water. It is thus considered a symbol of the human ability to discriminate between truth and falsehood, between fact and fiction.

Hamsa

The hamsa also symbolizes detachment in Hindu mythology, for although it lives in water, its feathers don't get wet. Thus it signifies someone who can live in the world without getting attached to it or seeking to control it, by simply accepting its flow. Sages are often called

Saraswati on a swan

param-hamsa or the great swan because of their ability to engage with the world without forming an attachment to it. The hamsa is also the vahana (mount) of Saraswati, the goddess of knowledge, as well as of Brahma, the god of creation. In Jainism, Saraswati is worshipped on her swan as the embodiment of Jina-vani, the wise speech of the Jina. In Buddhism, she transforms into Pragnya-Paramita, the embodiment of wisdom.

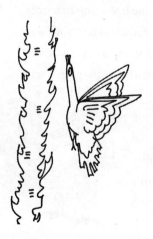

Brahma as a hamsa

Stories about the hamsa abound in mythology. The Hindu Puranas inform us that Brahma took the form of a hamsa to find the tip of a pillar of fire that extended into infinity. However, unable to locate the tip, he lied to the world that he had seen it, thus angering Shiva, who emerged from the pillar of fire and cursed Brahma that he would never be worshipped in temples.

In Buddhist literature, we are told the story of the hamsa who was shot dead in front of the Buddha by a hunter. The Buddha looked at the hunter and asked, 'Can you bring it back to life?' The hunter replied, 'No, I cannot.' The Buddha then said, 'If you cannot give life, what gives you the right to take life?'

In the Jataka tales, there is the story of a hamsa that gave one feather to a poor family every day. As soon as the feather touched the ground, it turned into gold and the family would use it to buy whatever they needed. Over time, the family became very rich – and greedy. One day they decided to catch the hamsa and pluck all its feathers, so they could become even richer. As they plucked the feathers of the trapped bird, they saw that the feathers were not turning into gold for they were being taken forcibly. This story perhaps travelled to other parts of the world and eventually became popular as the story of the goose that laid golden eggs.

This elegant arm-balance pose is visually similar to the Mayura-asana (Peacock pose), but with a few subtle differences. The arms are rotated 180 degrees so that the fingertips point forward. This position

Hamsa-asana   123

offers an increased element of difficulty as the weight of the legs tends to draw the body down and back and pressing into the fingers (usually the mechanism of control in arm balances) compounds this problem. Folding the legs into Padma-asana helps to bring the body's centre of gravity forward, and this in turn reduces the effort required to maintain the balance in this pose.

21

Marichi-asana
Marichi's Pose

When Brahma emerged from the lotus that rose from Vishnu's navel, he experienced the world for the first time. Finding himself alone, he experienced great fear and hunger. In order to make sense of the world, he moulded seven sons from his thoughts. These seven sons are rishis or seers. They observed the world and made sense of it and transmitted their knowledge in the form of hymns or chants, the collection of which is known as the Vedas.

Sapta Rishi

These seven rishis are associated with the Saptarshi or the Great Bear constellation. When they got married, they became Prajapatis, or progenitors of various races of beings. Marichi was one of the rishis. His son Kashyapa is the father of many celestial creatures including the birds, reptiles, fishes, animals with hooves and claws, the gods who live above the sky, and the asuras who live below the earth. That is why Brahma is called the great-grandfather of all living creatures and, since all worlds are connected to Brahma through his sons, the world is considered one big family, albeit an unhappy one where everyone fights over power and resources.

Marichi, Buddhist goddess of dawn

In the Bhagavad Gita, Krishna identifies Marichi as the foremost of the Maruts. The Maruts are wind gods, related to Vayu, and Marichi is the gentle breeze. This Marichi is unrelated to Marichi, the sage.

In Buddhist mythology, especially in China, Marichi is a guardian goddess, associated with dawn, light and sun, who rides a wild boar.

In Jain mythology, too, there is a Marichi. He is the son of Bharata, the ruler of earth, who in turn was the son of Rishabha, the first Jina of this eon. Marichi became a Jain monk and a great scholar. He would have become the Jina in the next life, however, he did not fully appreciate the Jain way, and so had to take rebirth several times, in several realms, once as a heroic Vasudev and another time as a Chakravarti king, before hc was finally reborn as the twenty-fourth Jina, Mahavira

This versatile seated posture has many variations consisting of both forward folds and revolved positions, and each is a progressive approach to increasing flexibility in the hips and spine. For versions of the pose that require folding a leg into Padma-asana, especially those that involve a seated twist, special attention should be paid to preserving the integrity of the knee joint. Practitioners who suffer from knee pain in Padma-asana can easily modify this series of postures by simply keeping the bent leg tucked underneath instead of folding it into a half lotus. Again, it is important to keep in mind that yoga-asana is a practice and not a performance. Forcing the body into positions it is not ready for stems from desire. I call it the 'look what I can do' complex, and this mentality not only results in frequent injury, but is essentially the opposite of why we do yoga in the first place. A good guideline to keep in mind when participating in any system of asana is to practice in such a way today so that we are able to do so again tomorrow. Overworking one's body is just as detrimental to our personal progress as underworking it is, if not more so.

———

22

Vasishtha-asana
Vasishtha's Pose

Vasishtha is one of the seven sages in Hindu mythology, who are represented in the sky as the Saptarshi or Great Bear constellation. It is said that when the Vedic gods Varuna and Mitra saw the beautiful damsel Urvashi, they lost control over their desires and spurted semen into a pot from which were born Vasishtha and Agastya. These stories allude to the belief that sages, who are celibate and perform various yogic practices, have semen so potent that it is able to rise upwards, through the spine and give them magical powers, as well as wisdom about the world. However, when shed, it transforms into a powerful being.

It is said that the seven sages had seven wives who were faithful to their husbands.

Birth of Vasishtha

The wives performed rituals around the fire regularly. Enchanted by the women, the fire god, Agni, tried to seduce them with his heat and light. Six of the wives fell under the spell of Agni, but the seventh, Vasishtha's wife, Arundhati, did not. She, therefore, sits beside the seven sages as the star Alcor in the Saptarshi constellation. The other six wives were cast out by their husbands and they became the Krittikas or the Pleaides constellation. Since then Arundhati has served as a symbol of wifely fidelity and womanly chastity.

Vasishtha is repeatedly mentioned in Vedic scriptures as the guardian of kings, and is Ram's teacher in the Ramayana. His rivalry with Vishwamitra is legendary. Vishwamitra killed many of Vasishtha's sons, but the latter never lost his temper. In fact, when his unborn child shouted from his mother's

Agni and the seven wives

womb that he would avenge his siblings' deaths, Vasishtha cautioned his son that anger did not solve any problems. This is an indicator of Vasishtha's patience, fortitude and wisdom.

Vasishtha told stories compiled in a book known as Yoga Vasishtha that explains how one can think like a hermit, while functioning as a householder. This knowledge enabled his student Ram, the prince of Ayodhya, to give up ideas of renunciation and take up the mantle of kingship.

The Yoga Vasishtha tells the story of the yogini Chudala whose husband refused to believe that a woman can be a master of yoga. He made her queen and went to the forest to learn yoga. Determined to make him see what he refused to acknowledge, Chudala followed him but she used her siddha powers to change her female body into that of a man called Kumbha. Her husband accepted Kumbha as a fellow seeker and the two practised yoga together. One night, Kumbha turned into a woman named Madanika and informed the husband that he had been cursed by a sage to become a woman every night. And since women were believed to be unable to control their desires, Kumbha-Madanika requested the husband to satisfy her sexually. 'But I am married and faithful to my Chudala,' said the husband. 'That's not a problem so long as you use your yogic training to detach your desires from servicing mine,' said Kumbha-Madanika. The husband did so, separating his mind from his body. A few nights later, the husband saw Kumbha in his Madanika form having sex with another man. He felt neither rage nor jealousy. A few days later, Indra came before the husband and offered him paradise, but the husband said, 'Paradise is in the mind not the body, inside not outside.' Indra then revealed that his companion, the man who became a woman at night, was actually his queen Chudala, who had followed him to the forest to make him look beyond gender. The husband, wiser now, accepted his wife as his teacher. They ruled the kingdom together.

Dedicated to the sage Vasishtha, this posture is all about extension. The longer and fuller the extension through the limbs, the easier it is to find and maintain one's balance. Progressions in this posture begin with simply finding the balance in a side plank position with the legs stacked together. Gradually over time, the top arm and leg can be lifted until a connection between the hand and toe becomes available. Postures like Supta Padangustha-asana (Reclined Big-toe pose) and the side variation of the same posture are excellent opportunities to work on the hip flexibility necessary for this full expression of Vasishtha-asana.

23

Durvasa-asana
Durvasa's Pose

Among all the rishis mentioned in the Hindu scriptures, Durvasa stands out because of his short temper. When Indra, king of the gods, did not acknowledge his presence as he was enjoying the dance of the apsaras, Durvasa cursed him that all his fortune would dissolve in the ocean of milk. It was finally restored when the gods churned the ocean of milk. When Shakuntala did not pay attention to Durvasa, as she was distracted by thoughts of her beloved, he cursed her that her lover, Dushyanta, would forget her. And Dushyanta does, because she loses the ring he gave her. Later, when he finds the ring, he remembers Shakuntala, but she is gone by then.

We often mistake knowledge with wisdom and assume that all the yogis and rishis are calm and composed beings with a permanent benign smile, like the Buddha or the Jina. However, in Hindu mythology, rishis are extremely knowledgeable men with a deep understanding of nature, who may or may not possess empathy, kindness or compassion. Of course, it is possible that sometimes this anger is a performance, part of a much bigger game.

Durvasa is one such being. He is a great scholar and possesses a lot of powers. These powers came to him through the practice of yoga and a thorough understanding of the world, which enable him to change the world. Such sages are known as Siddhis. The ability to change the world manifests in the form of boons and curses. Yogis are believed to have the powers to change karma. By granting a boon, they can bring good fortune, and by cursing they can bring misfortune in one's life. If life has a pattern created by karma, it can be changed by the intervention of a rishi.

In the Ramayana, Durvasa demands to see Ram. When told that the king has sought solitude in his private chambers, Durvasa threatens to curse the city of Ayodhya if Ram does not grant him an audience. Needless to say his wish was granted.

Durvasa cursing

In the Mahabharata, Durvasa is served by the princess Kunti so well that he gives the young princess a boon, that she can call any god at will and have a child by the deity. Kunti, unfortunately, uses this boon before marriage and bears a child whom she is forced to abandon on the river. Later, after her marriage, she uses the same boon to have children as her husband is unable to make her pregnant. Thus, Durvasa's boon enables Kunti to bear sons, the Pandavas, the heroes of the Mahabharata.

Durvasa was known as the 'angry sage' and had a reputation for having a very short temper. This posture gives the practitioner a little taste of that frustration as it quickly challenges one's balance, flexibility, strength and, subsequently, one's patience. Starting seated, one leg is brought into an Ekapada Shirsa-asana (Leg behind the Head pose), and the heel of the other foot is brought close to the hips. Then, very carefully, the standing leg begins to straighten while the torso is kept somewhat parallel to the floor. Once the balance is steady and consistent, the hands come together at the centre of the chest and the torso is then lifted on an inhaling breath. Generally, the supta ('supine' or 'reclined') variations of this posture, such as Bhairava-asana, are practised in order to achieve the necessary flexibility before one attempts to incorporate the balancing aspect of this pose.

24

Ruchika-asana
Ruchika's Pose

The rishis of Hindu mythology often married princesses. For example, the rishi Chyavana, associated with Ayurveda, married the princess Sukanya. It is said that while Chyavana was meditating, he stood still for so long that his body was covered with a termite hill. Sukanya happened to be passing by this termite hill and noticed two shiny objects within. Thinking they were fireflies, she poked at them, only to learn to her horror that they were Chyavana's eyes. Having blinded him, she was forced to become his wife, so she could take care

Chyavana in a termite hill

of him in his old age. She was a very dutiful wife. Pleased with her devotion, the gods transformed Chyavana into a youthful being and gave him the secret of Ayurveda, which enables people to stay youthful.

Chyavana's great-grandson, the sage Ruchika, also sought the hand of a princess named Satyavati in marriage. Satyavati's father, Gadhi, however, was reluctant to give his daughter to a hermit, who lived in the forest. Unable to say no, he asked something in return. He asked Ruchika for a magic potion that would enable him to father a son who would be a great warrior. Ruchika performed a ritual by which he created the magic potion and gave it to his father-in-law, saying that it would create a warrior son. Gadhi and his wife, however, doubted that such a child could be created by a sage. Meanwhile, Ruchika brewed another magic potion which would result in another child, a gentle son who would be a great sage. He gave the second potion to his wife, Satyavati. However, Satyavati

exchanged her pot with her mother because her mother believed that Ruchika would give a better magic potion to his wife than to his mother-in-law. As a result, the two women became pregnant, but since the pots had been exchanged Satyavati bore a child who would eventually choose to become a warrior

Ruchika and Satyavati

Yoga Mythology: 64 Asanas and their Stories

even though he was born in a family of sages, while her mother bore a son who would eventually choose to become a sage, even though he was born in a family of kings.

Gadhi thus became the father of Kaushika, a king, who gave up his kingdom to become Rishi Vishwamitra, and Satyavati bore a son called Jamadagni, who turned out to be a gentle soul; the magic potion manifested in the next generation. Jamadagni's son by the princess Renuka was Parshuram, who, though raised as a rishi, picked up the axe and hacked down the unrighteous kings of the earth.

This story reveals to us the magical powers associated with rishis. They had the ability to give children to childless women, and could even decide the personalities of the children.

This standing forward-bend asana adds an extra challenge to leg-behind-the-head postures by incorporating a one-legged standing balance. The asana is usually approached from a seated posture where the folded leg is put into position and then the practitioner comes to a standing half-forward fold position. Once the balance is stable, an exhaling breath brings the torso to fold over the standing leg. The subtle benefit of this posture is the altered positioning of one's centre of gravity as it differs from other standing forward bends. This, in turn, strengthens the balancing muscles of the legs and feet and ultimately provides an improved awareness (and control) of one's standing balance in general.

25

Vishwamitra-asana
Vishwamitra's Pose

Vishwamitra was once a king called Kaushika, who realized that the occult and mystical powers of rishis were far greater than the weapons, kingdom and military might that he possessed. So he decided to become a rishi and started performing various yogic practices. However, yoga demands complete sensory control and conquest of the restless mind. Since the gods did not want him to succeed, they sent the apsara Menaka to seduce him. Menaka succeeded very easily, angering Kaushika, who was determined to become a rishi at any cost. He continued his practice and though

Vishwamitra and Menaka

Indra kept sending nymphs to distract him, after his failure with Menaka, Kaushika developed so much control that he was able to ignore them and be indifferent to all of them. Eventually, he became so powerful that he came to be known as Vishwamitra.

Vishwamitra is famous for his rivalry with Vasishtha. He tried to kill Vasishtha's children but realized that Vasishtha never lost his temper and never sought retribution, revealing a wisdom that is the hallmark of a true yogi. Vishwamitra realized that a true yogi is not someone who is powerful, but someone who is wise.

Vishwamitra is known to test the integrity of kings by putting them through tough challenges. King Harischandra once disturbed Vishwamitra's yagna and to make amends offered him his kingdom. Vishwamitra accepted the apology and asked Harischandra to leave the kingdom. But when the king was leaving Vishwamitra said, 'The world will think you have given me the kingdom as charity or alms, not as an act of atonement. You must pay me a fee for helping you atone for your crime. That way I am not in your debt and you are not in mine.' Charity is called daan, alms are called bhiksha and service fee is called dakshina.

Harischandra demanding service fee

To pay the service fee, Harischandra who owned nothing now, was forced to sell his wife, son and himself as slaves in the market. Once king, he was reduced to being the servant of a crematorium-keeper. And his wife, once queen, became a kitchen maid. Some time later, their son, the prince, who also worked as assistant to his mother, was bitten by a snake and died. When his dead body was brought to the crematorium, Harischandra recognized his wife but demanded she pay the service fee for the cremation as required by his master; she would receive no special treatment. His wife owned nothing except the cloth she covered her body with. She offered it to him and he accepted. As she was disrobing, the gods descended from the heavens and praised Harischandra's integrity. As he had passed Vishwamitra's test, he was declared Indra, king of paradise.

In Sanskrit, visva means 'the world', but usually in a grand sense, so maybe a better translation would be 'the whole world'. Mitra means 'friend', and the long A vowel preceding it implies not just a friend, but a 'great friend'. Thus, this sage's name can be translated as 'Great Friend to the World'. Variations of this posture include the hand-foot connection as illustrated in the picture here or extending the top arm straight up and allowing the extended leg to point and float freely.

26

Galava-asana
Galava's Pose

When Kaushika gave up his kingdom and decided to become a hermit, he left his children in the care of his queen, hoping to return in a few months. However, months turned into years, for becoming a rishi is not easy. While he was away, a great drought struck the land. Kaushika's wife had no means to feed her children, so she decided to sell one of them. She tied a rope around her son Galava's neck and set out to take him to the market. But they were stopped by a prince, known as Satyavrata, who offered to feed them while Kaushika was away.

Galava on sale

When Kaushika returned as the great yogi Vishwamitra, he was so thankful

Trishanku

for Satyavrata's generosity that he offered the prince a boon. Satyavrata answered that he had been cursed that he would never be able to enter Indra's swarg, because he had accumulated too many demerits in his life. Vishwamitra promised to use his yogic powers to help Satyavrata enter Indra's paradise and so, he uttered all the magical mantras that enabled the prince to rise towards the heavens. However, Indra was very upset by this, since Satyavrata had not earned enough merit to enter heaven, so he pushed him back to earth. As a result, Satyavrata got stuck midway between the two worlds. He still hangs there, in this middle zone and is known as Trishanku, one who belongs neither here nor there.

Galava, eventually, became Vishwamitra's primary student and a great rishi. When his education was complete, Galava offered to give his father a gift, as did Vishwamitra's other students. Galava was following protocol as a student but Vishwamitra felt his son was mocking him, for having been more of a teacher and less of a father. 'Bring me a thousand white horses, each of which has one black ear,' said Vishwamitra. Galava went to King Yayati and asked for the same. The king said, 'These horses are rare, I have only two hundred. But I have a daughter who will bear four sons, destined to be kings, each one surely worth two hundred such horses to a childless king.' And so Galava went with the princess Madhavi and offered her womb to the kings who could give him two hundred white horses, each with one black ear. Madhavi managed to give three kings the sons they sought and in exchange Galava obtained six hundred horses, taking the total to eight hundred. No other king had similar horses. So he offered Madhavi's final child to Vishwamitra as equivalent to two hundred horses. 'That son can be king of the kingdom you abandoned when you became a sage.' Vishwamitra accepted Galava's eight hundred horses and Madhavi, pleased both as a father and teacher that Galava had achieved the impossible. Madhavi, mother of four kings by four different men, returned to her father, Yayati, who offered to get her married. However, Madhavi chose to be a hermit in the forest, perhaps disgusted by a world where a woman was valued more for her womb than for her heart or mind.

These stories of Vishwamitra speak of a time of great crisis in Vedic history, when parents sold their children for food and merit, sages and kings competed with each other to dominate society, and sons of kings became sages and sons of sages became warriors. Historians believe this was the age of the Upanishads, approximately the time when the monastic orders of Buddhism and Jainism rose and spread from the Gangetic plains to the eastern, southern and western parts of India.

This asana is dedicated to the sage Galava. In Sanskrit, gala means 'rope' or 'thread', and it is a direct reference to the rope by which Galava was brought to town to be sold by his mother. This posture has several variations such as the ekapada (one leg) version, pictured here, as well as the 'full' expression where both legs are folded into a lotus position and are then brought to rest behind one of the balancing arms. In some Western adaptations of asana practice, this posture is occasionally referred to as the 'Flying Pigeon' pose because, I assume, it has the same leg orientation as that of the Ekapada Raja Kapota-asana (One-legged Royal Pigeon pose), but this is something of a misnomer. When an asana name is altered, either for the sake of simplicity or due to an unwillingness to do one's research, it takes away from the richness and depth of the tradition, and eventually the mythological significance is (quite tragically) lost.

27

Ashtavakra-asana
Ashtavakra's Pose

Ancient Hindu philosophy comes from a set of scriptures, transmitted orally, known as the Vedas. These were chants that were put to melody and sung during a ritual known as the yagna. However, over time, people lost sight of the purpose of this ritual. Was it to invoke the gods and obtain boons and gifts from them, such as children and fertility, or was there divine wisdom about the nature of life embedded in the songs and the rites?

This prompted King Janaka of Mithila to organize a huge conference, where he invited sages from all over the land to discuss and reach a conclusion about the true nature of the Vedas and, more importantly, to help understand the true nature of the world. Sages came from far and wide. This gathering of sages, in Janaka's court, led to the composition of what we now call the Upanishads: discourses that try to explain the Hindu world view. The gathering of sages eventually inspired the famous Kumbha-mela, where wise men met to exchange pots of amrita, the nectar of immortality that represents knowledge.

One of the participants in Janaka's gathering was a sage called Kahoda. Before going to Janaka's palace, Kahoda was discussing the nature of the world and the nature of the Vedas with his wife, Sujata. Sujata was pregnant and the child, from within the mother's womb, corrected his father and pointed out flaws in his arguments. He did this eight times. The first seven times, Kahoda ignored his interruptions, but the eighth time, he got very angry and cursed the unborn child that since he had interrupted him eight times, he would be born with eight bends in his body. When the child was born, he was deformed, with eight twists in his body. Ashtavakra, as the boy was named, grew up to be an extremely intelligent boy. He enquired about his father and came to know his father had gone to King Janaka's court to discuss the true nature of the world; but there he had lost the debate. Kahoda had been condemned to die, having lost all prestige. In order to restore his father's honour, Ashtavakra went to Janaka's court and challenged the man who had defeated Kahoda. In the debate that followed, Ashtavakra very easily demonstrated his highly nuanced understanding of the Vedas and the Puranas. King Janaka and all the sages bowed to him. When offered a boon, he asked that his father's honour be restored and he be allowed to return home. Thus, Kahoda, who had punished his son for correcting him, rather than learning from him, realized his mistake and arrogance. Grey hair does not make one wiser, Ashtavakra told his father.

Ashtavakra is mentioned in the Ramayana and the Mahabharata, as well as in the Puranas. In the Ramayana, he is one of the sages who live in the forest. It must be kept in mind that in ancient India, there were many wise men who chose to live on the edge of a village or a forest, to understand the world better, over living in the city and serving kings. We could call them ancient-day philosophers, who were interested in understanding the nature of plants and animals. They speculated and organized many systems of knowledge such as Ayurveda, Tantra, yoga, linguistics and semiotics. Ashtavakra was clearly one of them. He is most renowned for his understanding of the atma, the human consciousness that is located within the body and around us. While the human body that has been given

Ashtavakra in Sujata's womb

to us by Brahma is hungry and is terrified of death, the atma is neither. Therefore, it becomes the source of tranquillity.

The fundamental difference between Buddhism and Hinduism is in the idea of the tranquil essence that is part of our being. Hindu yogis believe that the deepest essence of humanity is atma which is infinite and tranquil, while Buddhist yogis believe the essence is nothingness which grants tranquillity, for there is no entity called atma which resides in the body. Jainism accepts the idea of jiva-atma in all living organisms but rejects the idea of a cosmic param-atma.

Astau is the Sanskrit word for the number 'eight', and 'avakra' literally means 'not straight' or 'crooked'. In this context, the name of this asana is a direct reference to the sage's eight deformities of the limbs. Despite the complex appearance of this posture, it is actually one of the easier arm balances to work on as it is almost entirely reliant on bone support. The top leg is supported by the upper arm bone, the bottom leg is hooked on and supported by the top leg, and the weight of the body overall is supported by the vertical lower arm bones.

28

Kaundinya-asana
Kaundinya's Pose

There was a sage from India known as Kaundinya. This sage travelled across the sea to what was then called Suvarnabhumi, or the golden lands, where he met a Naga princess who was the ruler of the local people. The two got married. From them descended the Khmer kings of the kingdom of Kamboja, which later came to be known as Cambodia.

This idea of sages travelling across the sea, carrying ideas with them, from India, is widespread in South East Asia. These sages probably came along with seafaring merchants who took advantage of the monsoon winds for trade. India was famous for its fabrics and also for its stories. The high seas were also where leather puppets were invented and were used at night along with fire to create shadows on the sails of the ship to entertain sailors with stories from the Ramayana,

Mahabharata and the Jatakas. So, along the entire coast of India and South East Asia, one finds the stories of the previous lives of the Buddha and the great avatars of Vishnu, especially Ram, being depicted using leather puppetry. Indian languages and scripts also spread on these trade routes. In fact, Sanskrit became the royal language as far as Vietnam in the period between 300 CE and 1300 CE. And until the arrival of Islam, people in much of South East Asia venerated local gods alongside the Buddha, Shiva, Vishnu and Ram.

In Hindu mythology, Kaundinya does not play a very important role. He is merely one of the sages who accompanied Agastya to the south and then travelled beyond, taking Vedic culture with him. But Kaundinya plays a much bigger role in Buddhist mythology.

When Siddhartha Gautama is born in the Sakya clan, many sages predict that he will either become a sage who gives

Kaundinya

up the world and discovers wisdom or a great king who will conquer the world. Kaundinya is the only sage to insist that Siddhartha will not be a king, but a hermit, and he vows to be a follower of the hermit. Years later, when Siddhartha Gautama gives up his kingdom and goes to the forest and lives the hermit's life, Kaundinya and his students follow him. In Buddhist

Yoga Mythology: 64 Asanas and their Stories

literature, we are told that just as the Buddha had previous lives so did Kaundinya and they did engage with each other. In one story, the Buddha-to-be is a tiger and Kaundinya is a tigress and the Buddha-to-be offers his own life, so that the hungry tigress does not eat her own cubs.

In Jain mythology, before he renounced the world, the twenty-fourth Tirthankara of Jainism, Vardhamana Mahavira, was married to Yashodhara, who belonged to a clan that claimed descent from the sage Kaundinya. Yashodhara is also the name of the princess who married the prince of the Sakya clan who eventually became the awakened one or the Buddha. This sharing of names across the many mythologies of Indian origin reveals that these stories have common roots: either they are different trees of the same forest, or different branches of the same tree.

An intermediate arm-balance posture, Kaundinya-asana is a simple asana to find one's balance in, but it can be rather tricky to work the body into. There are generally three variations of this pose including two ekapada (one leg) and one dwipada (two legs).

The version pictured here is the second one-legged form of the posture. The arm balance and headstand entrances require a lot of core strength and coordination while the side plank entrance usually calls for a little more finesse. Controlling the posture, as with most arm balances, comes from pressing firmly into the floor with the fingertips and keeping the chin and chest raised upward.

29

Kashyapa-asana
Kashyapa's Pose

From Brahma's mind arose Marichi, whose son Kashyapa married many women, and through them became the progenitor of all living creatures. Through Aditi, he fathered the devas who live in the sky. Through Diti and Danu, he fathered the asuras, who live below the earth. Vinata gave birth to the birds, Kadru to the serpents, Surabhi to all hooved animals, Surasa to all clawed animals, and Timi to all sea creatures. Thus, all living beings, birds, fishes, reptiles, animal that graze, animals that hunt, creatures that live above

Kashyapa, father of all beings

the earth, creatures that live below the earth are connected by a common father called Kashyapa. We are all, eventually, descendants of Brahma. Vasudhaiva kutumbakam: the whole world is therefore my family.

But the reality of this family is that the children keep fighting with each other over resources in their quest for survival. Birds and snakes are in adversarial positions; snakes eat the eggs of birds and birds eat snakes. The devas who live in the sky have all the wealth in the world that the asuras below the earth seek. The devas feel entitled to their wealth and refuse to share it, while the asuras are jealous of what their half-brothers have. This leads to violent confrontation between the two. Interestingly, it is this conflict between the devas and the asuras that is responsible for creating the day and the night, summer and winter, the waxing and waning phases of the moon.

Kashyapa Buddha   Gautama Buddha   Maitreya Buddha
of the past   of the present   of the future

Kashyapa is visualized as a tortoise perhaps because the father of all creatures who quarrel constantly needs the patience and the withdrawal power of a tortoise.

While many Buddhists believe there is only one historical Buddha, in many Buddhist traditions, there were and will be many Buddhas in the world. If Siddhartha Gautama is the Buddha of present times, then Maitreya will be the Buddha of the future, while Kashyapa was the Buddha of the past. All of them were the awakened ones who told the world how to get rid of suffering. This idea of wisdom being eternal and being rediscovered and retransmitted from time to time is common to Buddhist, Jains and Hindus. These three faiths, based on eternity, limitlessness and rebirth, therefore call themselves sanatana dharma, or the timeless doctrine.

This blend of standing posture and arm balance offers a unique challenge to one's flexibility and balance. From a side plank position, the top leg is folded into Padma-asana while the top arm drapes around the back to grab the big toe. As the position becomes more stable, the gaze can be lifted skyward to encourage the opening of the chest and further challenge the practitioner's sense of balance. Postures like this that entail a side plank balance require strong engagement of the core musculature as well as an isometric lift of the midsection. Achieving this lift requires a subtle action through the side body that can be effectively described as the sensation of drawing the balancing hand and foot closer together.

30

Vajra-asana
The Thunderbolt Pose

Once upon a time, there was an asura called Vritra, who could not be defeated by anyone. So the devas went to Brahma and asked how they could defeat the asura. Brahma told them to create a weapon from a person who is completely detached. The devas wondered how they would find such a person. Brahma advised them to go around and talk to all the rishis, and ask which one of them would willingly give up his body, so that his bones – strengthened by years of meditation and austerities – could be used to create the most lethal of weapons.

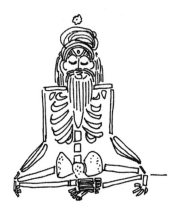

Dadhichi

Indra

The devas went all around the world and finally met a rishi called Dadhichi who willingly offered his body to Indra, king of the devas. He asked that his body be covered with salt. When this was done a cow came and licked the salt of his body, causing his flesh to separate from his bones. Thereafter the devas removed the bones, especially the vertebral column, from the remains and transformed them into a weapon known as the Vajra. This Vajra is Indra's thunderbolt, with which he finally defeated Vritra. It is said that this is the lightning that strikes monsoon clouds and releases rain.

Tantric Buddhism is called Vajrayana Buddhism, the lightning path. It is practised in the Himalayan regions of Tibet and Bhutan. Here rituals play an important role; awakening into Buddhahood is seen as an 'accident', striking us as lightning strikes the earth, and rituals make us 'accident-prone'. The Buddha and deities such as Vajrapani and teachers like Padmasambhava are often shown holding a thunderbolt in one hand and a bell in the other, embodying the male and female principles of life – the mind within and the body without, the compassion and the wisdom.

Vajra Tara

Since the eighth century, Mahayana and Tantric Buddhism have accommodated Tara, goddess of wisdom, who complements the Buddha's compassion. There are many Taras, including Vajra Tara, or thunderbolt Tara. She is visualized holding the thunderbolt and bell as well as knives and skulls. She is sometimes called Vajra-yogini and Vajra-varahi, each a fierce manifestation of human consciousness.

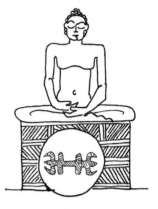

Jina Dharma-nath

The Vajra is also the symbol of the fifteenth Jina of this eon, Dharma-nath.

Vajra is the Sanskrit word for 'lightning bolt' and may be a reference to the jagged shape of the body when the pose is viewed from the side. A relatively complicated posture, Vajra-asana requires deeply folding the legs into Padma-asana and then grabbing opposite toes from behind one's back. Once the bind with the toes is achieved, one slowly lowers on to the back until the arms and head are in contact with the floor. In some asana traditions, this posture is usually worked on with the aid of an assistant who places their legs over those of the practitioner. This additional weight provides a firm foundation from which the back-bending portion of the asana becomes easier.

Shiva

S hiva is called the destroyer. However, the word 'destroyer' has a negative connotation, which is why many people say Shiva is the destroyer only of 'evil' forces. But that would make Brahma the creator of evil forces, and Vishnu the preserver of evil forces. The question one needs to ask is what does Shiva destroy that makes him worthy of worship, and what does Brahma create that makes him unworthy of worship.

Evil is not an Indic notion; it is an idea found in one-birth mythologies where there is no concept of karma. Karma means that every event, good or bad, has a cause and a consequence. Hunger for food and fear of death are both the cause and consequence of life; together they rotate the wheel of karma. Hunger and fear make humans establish cultures with rules and responsibilities. Hunger for meaning and the fear of invalidation drives humans to hoard wealth and power, create inequality and establish hierarchy, which results in conflict.

Indra

Brahma's creations, his progeny, embody all these qualities. His 'most successful' grandchild, Indra, king of the devas, has everything one could desire in paradise, from the wish-fulfilling tree, cow and jewel to the nectar of immortality. But though prosperous, Indra has no peace. He is forever fighting his half-brothers, the asuras, also grandchildren of Brahma, who feel they have been cheated out of what is rightfully their share of wealth. This makes Brahma, who indulges hunger and fear, the creator of culture as well as conflict. And this makes him unworthy of worship.

Shiva destroys the god of desire, Kamadeva, and defeats the god of death, Yama, and so is called Kamantaka and Yamantaka. His indifference to property and pleasure also makes him destroy culture. As he outgrows hunger and fear, he ends all conflict and brings peace. Shiva is therefore worshipped. He embodies the great ascetic traditions of India. He is the primal ash-smeared hermit with dreadlocks who walks around the world with a snake slithering

Kama

around his neck. Occasionally clad in animal hide, he carries a trident and a rattle drum, to remind all humans how we are trapped in the world, and how our mind jumps around like a monkey. He smokes narcotics that help the mind move away from mundane reality and sense the world more clearly, more slowly.

Yama

Shiva reminds us of Buddhist and Jain monks and teachers who give up desire and transcend the cycle of rebirth. Indeed the first Jain Tirthankara, Rishabha, has a bull as his symbol, just like Shiva. Rishabha attained omniscience atop Mount Kailas, which is known to Hindus as the abode of Shiva. But there is a difference. Shiva is not just a hermit, he is also a householder. The Goddess asks Shiva what use this wisdom is if it cannot be shared with others. And so, she compels him to marry, descend from his mountain abode, become a father,

and engage with the world. Shiva's 'eroticism' that titillates many in a rather juvenile way is the metaphor of the withdrawn mind being made to engage with the body and the world at large. Shiva is worshipped as he abandons his desolate abode atop icy mountains and lives as a householder with people in the river plains below, making his wisdom accessible to all.

Shakti

The Goddess makes the silent Shiva reveal the secrets of the universe through discourses, dance and music. Shiva has so much wisdom that he is also called Bhole Nath, the gullible one, for he fails to understand human rules and the obsession with power and property. The tension between Shiva and his wife Shakti is the tension between wisdom and pragmatism, the soul which is never hungry or frightened, and the flesh that needs to be fed, protected and nurtured. The Vedanta school of Hinduism places greater emphasis on Shiva's rather masculine hermit side; in Tantra, the greater emphasis is on Shiva's householder side shaped by Devi, the material, and the feminine.

The transformation of Buddhism from Theravada (the path of elders) to Mahayana (the greater path) resonates the transformation of hermit Shiva into householder Shiva, for Mahayana Buddhism acknowledges the feminine as the goddess Tara, and values 'feminine' traits like compassion (karuna) embodied in the Bodhisattva. Mahayana Buddhism became popular in Central Asia and China, where the king was seen as the Bodhisattva who takes care of his people. Theravada Buddhism maintained its popularity in Burma, Sri Lanka and Thailand, where the king was seen as the defender of the Buddha's doctrine

31

Parvata-asana
The Mountain Pose

Shiva sits atop Mount Kailas which is a mountain covered with snow. It evokes stillness. Parvati, the daughter of the mountains, gets him to become her husband. She releases the 'heat' within him that has caused everything around him to freeze. This 'heat' takes the form of knowledge, and the arts, and even rivers that flow down from him, like the Ganges.

This idea of the union of male and female metaphors that balance the spiritual and the material is resonated in the Yab–Yum (father–mother) images of Tibetan Tantric Buddhism too. Goddess Tara sits on the lap of the Bodhisattva and copulates with him. By being on top, she evokes volition. The hermit is thus forced to acknowledge the world

Parvata

Shiva and Shakti atop
Mount Kailas

of householders. The sexual act becomes a metaphor for engagement with material reality. The seated yogi, like the mountain, is abstracted to an upright triangle; the yogini, like a waterfall, is abstracted to a downward pointing triangle.

Mount Kailas is made of stone and covered with ice; nothing grows there and so there is no food to eat. Yet Shiva lives here, with his entire family and his followers, who have outgrown all desire. For those who follow Shiva have no hunger.

There are many important mountains in Indic mythology, the most significant being Mount Meru – sometimes called Mount Mandar. It is believed to be the centre of the world. In Buddhist mythology, the thirty-three devas sit on top of Mount Meru, while the asuras live at the base of this mountain. Continents spread out from this mountain like the petals of a lotus flower.

In Jainism, all the Jinas attain omniscience atop mountains, hence Jain temples and monasteries are typically located atop mountains, and are built with four gates facing the four directions to evoke the idea of

Jina Rishabha-nath atop
Mount Kailas

all-seeing wisdom. In India, the temples of guardian gods and goddesses are situated on mountain tops.

This idea that mountains that scraped the sky were the abode of the gods is found in Greek mythology too. Even in the Bible, the word of God comes to the world of humans down the slopes of Mount Sinai.

The Hindu Puranas state that mountains once had wings and could fly across the sky like clouds. But then, they started sitting on trees, imagining themselves to be birds, and that caused the branches of the trees to fall on sages below. The sages got angry and tore off the wings of the mountains. Since then they have been stuck on the ground, visited by clouds that mourn the days when they could fly together.

A parvata is a 'mountain' in Sanskrit, and though not what most practitioners identify as the Mountain pose, this could be considered an advanced progression of Tada-asana, a variant of the pose.

This particular asana variation (from the Ashtanga Vinyasa tradition) provides a unique approach to standing balance, where normally one's weight is distributed between the front and back of the foot; this posture requires distribution between the inner and outer edges of the feet. Usually approached from a bent-leg standing position, the heels are brought together, and the toes are then turned outward. From there, the legs gradually straighten with the hips in a full external rotation. As always, practice and patience are a yogi's best friend and it may be helpful to work on some seated-hip openers for a range of motion before working on this tricky balance. Additionally, practicing while facing a wall can be helpful while one is developing this new sense of weight distribution. Another variation of this asana (stemming from the Iyengar tradition) is a cross-legged seated posture with the fingers interlaced and arms extended overhead.

32

Siddha-asana
The Pose of the Accomplished

In Jain mythology, the highest heaven outside the wheel of rebirth is Siddha-loka, where the Jinas reside. They are the accomplished ones, those who have broken free from all material reality and are immersed in spiritual reality, and are all-knowing and all-powerful.

Jainism believes liberating the soul (jiva) from material entrapments and realizing spiritual reality is the goal of Jain yoga. Buddhism rejects the existence of the eternal soul; the realization of essential nothingness (shunya) is the goal of Buddhist yoga. Hinduism insists on the idea of God, a cosmic soul, the union with whom is the goal of Hindu yoga. Yet, all three faiths speak of siddha.

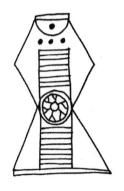

The Jain world

Siddha has more do with the occult than with mysticism. The occult explores the ability to control material reality through spiritual reality. The mystical focuses on the ability to break free from material reality and unite with spiritual reality. The occult has more to do with magic, and mysticism has more to do with wisdom.

With siddha, the yogi can leave his own body, enter and animate dead bodies, experience life differently, and return to the original body. It gives him the ability to change his size, his shape, walk on water, fly in air, and perform various feats like bringing down rain and enabling childless women to bear children. Siddhas were considered sorcerers, valued greatly across India for their knowledge of medicine, their understanding of astrology, and their ability to harness good luck and positive energy for the benefit of the household.

A siddha can choose death, and voluntarily leave his body. This act is called 'samadhi' in many yogic schools, for it is seen as a union with the cosmic soul. A body thus abandoned

Shiva meditating on Mount Kailas

voluntarily is considered auspicious, and is therefore buried and worshipped, rather than cremated and forgotten. Cremation, a common Hindu and Jain practice, is for people whose death was involuntary; who are trapped in the wheel of rebirth. The siddha is free of this wheel. He is limited neither by his body nor by nature.

His tomb is also referred to as samadhi, and visited by those seeking to change their material circumstances.

Siddha is strongly linked with Tantra and semen power, the occult belief that human males have the power to withhold semen and even reverse its direction, making it move up the spine until the powers hidden in the brain are unlocked. Shiva is the primal siddha and so he has a third eye. Hanuman is also a siddha, a drop of whose sweat can make a fish pregnant. Matsyendra-nath and Gorakh-nath are both siddhas and are thus able to resist the curse of the enchanted banana forest that turns all men into women.

Hanuman, the siddha

The hermit Shankara (a historical figure, not to be confused with the mythological Shankara, the householder form of Shiva), one of India's greatest Vedic philosophers who lived some twelve centuries ago, defeated Mandana Mishra, the householder, in a debate. Mandana Mishra's wife, Ubhaya Bharati, then asked Shankara if he could throw some light on matters related to sex and pleasure. Shankara said that as a hermit he had stayed away from such knowledge and experience. 'How then can you claim to have knowledge of

Siddha

the universe?' she argued. She was right, of course. Shankara wondered how he could gain that knowledge without breaking his vow of celibacy and continence. Finally, yoga came to his rescue: he was able to take his mind out of his body and enter the body of a king called Amaru who had just died. Through Amaru's reanimated body he was able to experience sex and all kinds of pleasure. Shankara returned to his virginal body enlightened, after gaining enough knowledge and experience.

Nearly twelve centuries before Shankara, the Buddha had warned his students not to take advantage of these magical abilities and to keep them secret, except in the pursuit of further knowledge, and at best for self-defence or during an emergency. And so when many of the Buddha's students learnt that he had passed away, they used their siddha powers to transport themselves rapidly across great distances to attend his funeral ceremony. The Buddha's bones were, however, not cast in the river as he would never be reborn; they were instead kept as relics in stupas, to be adored and worshipped.

Death of the Buddha

Although today the trend is to value the mystical yogi, it is the occult yogi with magical powers who was deemed very important in traditional society and folklore. Even today, many people insist that their gurus have magical powers. In fact, for many people spirituality is less about psychology and more about the paranormal and the magical.

Siddhi is the Sanskrit word for 'enlightenment' and is perhaps a reference to the posture's use for the practice of dhyana (focus). This asana offers the widest base for a crossed-leg seated position and is therefore among the most stable. This quality makes it the ideal seat for maintaining one's posture in pranayama (regulating the flow of the breath) and other forms of dharana (perspective). And here, I think, there is an important distinction to be made. In the West, the 'practice of yoga' is very much focused on the physical aspects of the yoga system. The Ashtanga yoga system, as prescribed by Patanjali, is a systematic approach to meditation. The practice of asana, which literally translates to 'sitting', was only designed and intended as a method of preparing the body for long periods of seated meditation, and nothing more, on the path to samadhi, which comes from the conjunction of the Sanskrit words sama, meaning 'even', and dhi, which is a reference to the 'higher mind'. This 'evenness of the higher mind' is the true end-goal of yoga, and to attain it is called siddh, 'to become enlightened' or 'empowered'. This then gives us context to better understand the word siddhi, from which this posture acquires its name.

33

Bhairava-asana
The Pose of the Fear-remover

Shiva sat silent with his eyes shut atop Mount Kailas when he was awakened by the cries of the Goddess, who was being chased by Brahma. The creator, on his first sight of the Goddess, was so enamoured by her that he kept staring at her, until he grew four more heads. Disgusted by this display of desire, Shiva took the form of Bhairava, caught hold of Brahma, and severed his fifth head with his sharp nails.

By cutting off Brahma's fifth head, Bhairava brought him to his senses, and forced him to reconsider his actions. Brahma's mind then started creating his mind-born sons, the rishis, who saw the world for what it is rather than what Brahma wanted it to be. They saw how Brahma was trying to control and possess the world, that he was falling victim to hunger and fear. They were being created simultaneously to help resolve the situation. The rishis then discovered the method by which one can outgrow hunger and fear – yoga. They dedicated their learning to Shiva who is Bhairava, the one who initiated the removal of fear in Brahma.

In Indic mythology, multiple heads refer to increasing knowledge and sensitivity, which is why many Bodhisattvas of Buddhism have several heads. It also indicates knotting of the mind and the rise of the ego, as in the story of Brahma's fifth head. His transformation from a one-headed god to a five-headed god

Heruka with Yogini

indicates Brahma increasing desire to consume and possess his creation. Thus, it evokes attachment. Words like 'mine' and 'yours' are human inventions to claim ownership over nature. Bhairava mocks such behaviour and sees it as the creation of the human ego which seeks meaning in possessions. Shiva wrenches out Brahma's fifth head, the arrogance that often follows knowledge.

Bhairava

Having beheaded Brahma, it is said that Shiva became impure and inauspicious. He wandered around the world, carrying Brahma's severed head which is seared into his own flesh. This is why he is also called Kapalika or the skull-bearing sage. In Kashi, finally, Brahma's skull falls off. Therefore, Shiva, the hermit, becomes the guardian of Kashi, and is called the policeman (kotwal) of Kashi. The city is also the home of the Goddess, where she takes the form of Annapurna, or the one who feeds the people. Thus Bhairava is the guardian of the Goddess – the one who attacks those who try to control and claim possession over the Goddess.

Images of Bhairava as guardian are found not just in Hindu temples but also in Jain temples.

Bhairava is also a fierce Buddhist deity, a dhamma-pala, or protector of Tantric Buddhism. Also known as Heruka, Mahakala and Yamantaka, this is clearly a syncretic deity once found across parts of east India, from Odisha to Bengal, and thence to the Himalayan kingdoms of Nepal, Bhutan, Sikkim and Tibet. He is often visualized as copulating with a Tara (Shakti of Hinduism). While Buddhist Tara is always diminutive with respect to Bhairava, Hindu Shakti is often visualized as larger and served by her Bhairava.

In Sanskrit, the word bhaya means 'fear'. Bhairava means 'remover of fear' and is one of the 1000 names of Shiva (who removes the fear of death). This reclined posture represents the pacified

Shiva while the more intense arm-balance version of this asana, Kala Bhairava-asana, represents the destructive aspect of Shiva. Offering a deep stretch to the outer hips, this posture takes quite a bit of practice to work up to. Seated hip-openers such as Baddha Kona-asana (Bound Angle pose) and Agni Stamba-asana (Fire Log pose) can be helpful preparation postures.

———

34

Svana-asana
The Dog Pose

If the Goddess is associated with the cat, Shiva is associated with the dog, especially in his fearsome Bhairava form. One can say that the Goddess embodies an independent spirit, while Shiva does not. However, that is not quite accurate, because Shiva is also associated with the wild bull, which cannot be domesticated and must be left alone in the field; the bull is useful only to impregnate the cow, but useless to pull a plough or a cart. So, what does the dog represent and why is it so closely associated with Shiva?

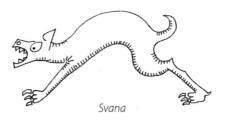

Svana

The reason is that the dog is considered an inauspicious animal in Hinduism, associated with crematoriums and garbage, and is kept outside the house. It also embodies fear, because the dog barks when it is frightened and wags its tail when it seeks approval. Thus, it is a metaphor for the insecurity that is destroyed by Shiva, which is why Shiva, in his Bhairava form, is associated with the dog. Also, like a dog, Bhairava is the protector of the Goddess.

Hadkai-mata

The Vaghri Dev Pujak community of Gujarat in western India paints images of their goddesses on cloth. They worship Hadkai-mata, the goddess who rides a dog and protects them from rabies.

In the mythology of Nath yogis, Bhairava transforms into the gentle Dattatreya, who is associated with four dogs that are more like gentle puppies, considered to be the four Vedas or the four Shastras. The dogs walk ahead of him, constantly turning around to see if the master is following them. Shiva thus embodies the wisdom that calms the frightened dogs of our mind.

In a tale from the Jatakas, the king of Varanasi finds that the leather harness of his chariot has been chewed and torn by dogs. He orders that all the dogs of the city, except those of the palace, be killed. A dog from the crematorium, that is actually the Buddha-to-be reborn, enters the king's court and asks him to prove that it was the dogs from the city, and not the palace, who damaged the harness. The king has no proof but the Buddha-to-be makes the royal dogs vomit and reveals leather in their stomach contents. The dog thus teaches the king the value of proof in matters of justice.

Quite possibly the two most aptly named postures are the Upward and Downward Facing Dog poses. Svana is the Sanskrit word for 'dog'. These postures are named for their obvious resemblance to the way dogs stretch their front and hind legs. The asanas usually have descriptors attached to indicate which variation of the asana is being performed: specifically, urdhva mukha, meaning 'upward-facing', and adho mukha, meaning 'downward-facing'. The variation depicted here is the upward-facing one that is usually conducted in the opening sequence of the Surya Namaskar as a general warm-up, or sometimes as a precursor to other back-bending postures.

───────────────

35

Virabhadra-asana
The Pose of the Righteous Warrior

Before Shiva was domesticated and transformed from a hermit to a householder by the goddess Parvati, princess of the mountains, he was married to Sati. Sati had chosen Shiva as her husband much against the wishes of Daksha, her father. A puritanical priest who performed rituals, Daksha

felt that Shiva was an unworthy groom because he did not perform any rituals or have a vocation or any possessions, and because he wandered the world like a vagabond, in the company of ghosts, goblins and dogs, making him inauspicious.

Virabhadra, holding Daksha's head

When Sati chose to marry Shiva against her father's wishes, a furious Daksha organized a yagna and invited all the gods except Shiva to receive offerings. This angered Sati, and she stormed her father's sacrificial hall and offered herself as the sacrifice in the great fire. Daksha, however, was unmoved by his daughter's death and continued with the ritual as if nothing had happened.

When news of Sati's death reached Shiva, he became so enraged that he transformed into Virabhadra, the righteous warrior. Virabhadra marched with an army of ghosts and goblins into Daksha's ritual hall, broke the pots, burned the tapestries and destroyed the entire ritual. Finally he beheaded Daksha. Thus Virabhadra is always depicted wielding a sword in one hand and carrying the severed head of Daksha in the other.

The gods begged Shiva for mercy, and Shiva, who is known to be quick to anger but also easy to pacify, calmed down and restored Daksha to life by giving him a new head – that of a goat, so he would realize that territorial behaviour and possessiveness are qualities best suited to animals. Humans should not be possessive about the things they have; they must let them go, or pass them on in the spirit of generosity. Daksha had failed to display that generosity. He was attached to his daughter and did not give her autonomy and therefore was unworthy of being a leader of humanity.

The conflict between Daksha and Shiva is also a conflict between orthodox Vedic traditions based on strict rules and hierarchy, and radical Tantric traditions that reject all rules and hierarchy. In the former, the Goddess is daughter, in the latter the Goddess is mother. In Vedanta, the Goddess is seen as both maya (delusion) and vidya (knowledge that helps us overpower delusion). In Tantra, the Goddess is shakti, power. Daksha is trapped in maya; Shiva is associated with vidya and shakti.

Across India, we find many village deities depicted brandishing a sword and accompanied by a dog. These are often identified as Virabhadra, the guardian form of Shiva. Virabhadra seems similar to Bhairava but is less wild. In art, Bhairava is sometimes visualized as being childlike but not Virabhadra, who always sports a moustache. Bhairava is sometimes depicted naked and is therefore deemed indecent (abhadra), unlike the more decently covered Virabhadra. In a similar vein, Kali is called Bhadrakali when she covers her nakedness and becomes more accessible to culture.

The story of Virabhadra is represented by three separate postures that each depict a specific aspect of the legend. The first form represents the manifestation of Shiva's rage as he becomes the terrifying Virabhadra. The second form of the posture is symbolic of Virabhadra beheading Daksha after the loss of his beloved Sati. The final form represents Virabhadra holding the severed head out over the sacrificial fire as an offering, but it can also be interpreted as the act of reviving Daksha by placing the goat head on the decapitated body. Vira means 'hero' and bhadra means 'righteous' or 'decent' in Sanskrit.

_____

36

Nataraja-asana
The Dancer Pose

S hiva is associated with both stillness and with movement. As the still hermit, he sits atop a mountain, immobile, eyes shut, withdrawn from the world. But when he is brought down to the plains by his wife Parvati, inspired by her, he becomes the dancing householder, Nataraja. The world of Shiva is beyond space (desha), time (kala), rupa (form) and name (nama), whereas the world of Shakti is within these limitations. The journey from stillness to movement, from the mountain top to the plains is the journey from the world of Shiva to the world of Shakti.

Nataraja

Once, a group of ascetics was performing rituals, unaware of their true significance or purpose. The sages used these rituals to become powerful and control the world. Shiva approached them as a naked ascetic. He was so handsome that the wives of the sages ran after him, angering their husbands who accused him of trying to seduce their wives. From the fire pit and the rituals, they chanted occult mantras to create a tiger, a serpent and a goblin to defeat Shiva.

Shiva, very calmly, flayed the tiger alive and wrapped himself in the beast's skin. He picked up the venomous serpent and coiled him around his neck. Then he kicked the demon down on the ground and danced on his back. As he danced, his hands and legs and fingers moved in such a way that the people watching him realized he was not merely dancing for his pleasure, but was communicating through the gestures. This communication revealed to them the wisdom of the Vedas.

Dance of Shiva

The Vedas are not about the power to indulge hunger and fear but about the knowledge and wisdom that help us overcome hunger and fear. Therefore, the pose of Nataraja is very sacred in Hinduism. If one studies this visual carefully, one understands the Vedas without needing to understand the written word.

We must understand that for a long period, in India, literacy was not important. Oral and visual traditions mattered more than written traditions. The Nataraja image is a symbolic visual depiction of a choreographed performance of Indic wisdom, where the moving hand and feet represent the world, which is continuously changing. Shiva holds up his hand in the abhaya mudra, with the palm facing outwards, telling us not to be afraid of his moving foot but to focus on the still foot on the ground which represents the soul. The soul is neither created nor destroyed. It is immortal; therefore, it is neither hungry nor does it fear death. It is our true essence as far as yoga philosophy is concerned.

In Buddhist traditions, beyond the transitory world there is nothingness (shunya) and the experience of nothingness is considered wisdom. In Hinduism, the opposite is true: beyond the ever-changing material world is the experience of infinity (ananta) which is embodied in Shiva, the hermit, and Vishnu, the householder.

The blazing ring of fire around the dance of Shiva is the wheel of rebirth (samsara). The demon on whose back Shiva dances is the demon of ignorance and imagined memories (apasmara). Thus Shiva is also called Smarantaka, one who destroys ignorance and imagined memories, unknotting the mind until it realizes its pristine primal form. This same dance inspired Patanjali to write the Yoga-sutra (a treatise on the mind) and Bharata to write the Natyashastra (a treatise on dance).

In traditional Indian dance, 'tandava' also refers to the masculine robust form of dancing, which is complemented by 'lasya', the feminine seductive form of dancing usually performed by the more worldly Vishnu. Nata is one of the many Sanskrit words for 'dance', raja means 'royalty' or 'king'. This posture represents one of the most powerful and beautiful ideas in all of yoga mythology – that when it is written down, an idea exists in space, and in time when it is spoken aloud, but when it is conveyed through a dance, it exists in both time and space, and that is why it is representative of Mahadeva, 'the greatest god'. This idea also carries the quality of uniqueness in that no two dances are ever exactly the same, and, similarly, no two asana practices can ever be the same. Embracing this idea gives us perspective and appreciation for what is happening right now, in this moment, because it is impossible to ever recreate or duplicate any experience exactly.

37

Shava-asana
The Corpse Pose

In Shakta mythology, or the mythology of the Goddess, Shiva is actually shava – a dead body – until the goddess Kali dances on him. Without the Goddess, he is as good as a corpse. This popular story embodies the dichotomy between matter and the mind, or matter without the soul. Words like mind (mana), soul (atma), spirit (jiva) and consciousness (chitta) are all used interchangeably, depending on the context.

Only when the soul enters the body does it become alive and experience hunger and fear and the desire to live. The soul, which by itself is disembodied and has no form, is sometimes called a ghost (bhuta). Shiva is considered the lord of the ghosts (Bhuteshwara): the spirit without substance. The Goddess is believed to be substance without spirit. Only when the two come together is life created. Thus, the shava transforms into Shiva only when the Goddess intervenes.

One of the greatest discussions in Hindu mythology is which is superior: the spirit or matter. Did matter come first and then the spirit, or did the spirit come first and then matter? Who creates whom? There is always a tussle between the two. It is very significant that the spirit, or the disembodied life force, is given a masculine form, while the body – male or female – is associated

Kali atop Shiva

with the Goddess and the feminine nature of things. In Hindu mythology, the female metaphor represents material reality: everything that is bound by space and time, everything that has a boundary and has a form and therefore a name. The disembodied life force, consciousness or imagination is represented through male metaphors. These defy the limits of space and time. We can imagine the past and future without being physically present in either. We can imagine other worlds without moving out of the one we currently inhabit.

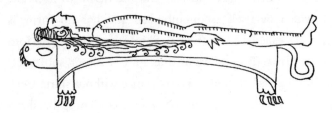

Shiva as shava

Brahma, Vishnu and Shiva represent the disembodied spirit in various stages. Brahma represents the hungry spirit, seeking meaning; Shiva, the wise spirit that does not seek meaning, but also does not engage with the rest of the world; and Vishnu, the wise spirit with meaning that engages with the world. But none of the three gods can function unless the world exists and they have a body through which they can communicate with the world. Both the body and the world are visualized as the Goddess. He needs her to sense himself; she needs him to enliven her.

I often hear this posture being referred to as the 'most difficult posture to achieve', but I don't necessarily agree. Some schools of yoga teach Shava-asana differently from the restful position of repose that it is usually offered as. In Sanskrit, shava means 'corpse' and in certain lineages of the yoga tradition, Shava-asana is done by holding the body extremely rigid (such as when rigor mortis sets in on a corpse). Some depictions of the posture even show the practitioner atop two blocks, one supporting the back of the head and the other supporting the ankles while the rest of the body is suspended above the ground, like a board placed on top of two supports. Personally, I tend to offer this position as a completely relaxed and restful means of release after what is usually a rather challenging and rigorous physical routine. However, there are valid arguments to both approaches. In my opinion, the most successful Shava-asana is the one that leaves the practitioner calmer and more centred than when they initially entered the pose.

———————

38

Skanda-asana
Skanda's Pose

While the world was being threatened by the asura Taraka, Shiva sat still, atop Mount Kailas, his eyes shut, his mind focused inward; all heat was contained within his body and the world around him turned into ice. Taraka had sought a boon that only a six-day-old child could kill him, an impossible condition that ensured his invincibility. However, the gods figured out that Shiva could father a child powerful enough to, on the sixth day after his birth, go into battle and defeat Taraka, for he had practised yoga for thousands of years. So, they

Kartikeya

begged the Goddess, Shakti, to marry Shiva and make him father a child.

The Goddess managed to convince Shiva to get married and they engaged in sexual intercourse, but Shiva showed no interest in ejaculation. Finally, the gods had to disturb the divine love-making, causing Shiva to lose his concentration and spurt his semen. Unfortunately, the semen fell not inside the Goddess's womb, but outside, and had to be collected by the fire god, Agni.

Shiva's semen was so hot that even the fire god could not bear it, so he passed it on to the wind god, Vayu, but even the wind god couldn't cool it down. So, it was thrown into a river that began to boil, setting aflame the reeds on the riverbank. When the fire died down, it revealed six children, in the shape of six lotus flowers. They were nursed by the six-star goddesses of the Pleiades constellation known as Krittika, from which comes the name Kartikeya.

Later, the Goddess, Shakti, came and took the six children and merged them into a single child. This child received many names, including Skanda. Skanda is visualized as a great god who holds a lance in his hands and rides a peacock when he goes into battle. He led the forces of the gods in battle against Taraka and defeated him.

Kartikeya is the warrior of the gods, sponsor of royal armies, though he is often imagined as a child or boy, hence the name Kumara. He embodies Shiva's world-engaging form, because the ascetic Shiva does not engage with the world. Shiva's son does the needful by protecting the world. While in north Indian traditions Skanda is a celibate warrior riding a peacock, in south Indian traditions, where he is often called Murugan, he stands on a mountain top and has two wives, the celestial daughter of Indra, Sena, and the earthy tribal beauty, Valli. In east India, he is pictured as the sports-loving patron of the arts who loves the good things in life, like the landed gentry of yore, and quite unlike his more studious, sedentary, pot-bellied elephant-headed brother. Thus we see how Hindu mythology has variants within India itself.

Linked to the planet Mars in astrology, Skanda has often been compared to Ares, the Greek god of war. Some say that his name, Skanda, inspired the Indian name Sikandar for Alexander the Great.

Skanda is another name for Kartikeya, the warrior of the gods and brother to the elephant-headed god, Ganesha. Both are sons of Shiva. And like Kartikeya, this posture represents a struggle for victory, achievement and overcoming of obstacles as the practitioner works towards a deeper and fuller expression of the asana. Generally considered a progression from the initial position of Ekapada Shirsa-asana (one leg behind the head), this pose is entered from a seat by placing the leg behind the head and then taking a full forward extension over the straight leg. The binding of the wrists (the hand on same side as the bent leg generally grabs the other hand) is the final movement, but the work doesn't stop there. Each successive inhale offers an opportunity to lift and lengthen the spine forward, and each subsequent exhale provides an opportunity to fold a little further into the pose. Given the nature of the deity after whom the pose is named, sometimes this posture is referred to as the God of War.

39

Shanmukhi Mudra-asana
The Six-faced Seal Pose

S anmukha (the one with six heads) is another name for the powerful Kartikeya. Shiva's other son, the elephant-headed Ganesha, in contrast to Kartikeya, is associated with affluence, abundance and learning. If Sanmukha erases fear, then Ganesha takes away hunger. Together, these sons of Shiva grant us liberation from all that entraps us.

While the Puranas, which are some 1500 years old, speak of Kartikeya as the son of Shiva and Shakti, older texts, such as the Mahabharata, dated over 2000 years, describe Kartikeya as the son of Agni, the fire god, who desired the seven wives of the seven celestial sages (Sapta Rishis). However, only six of the women succumbed to Agni's charms and became pregnant, simply from contact with the fire's heat and light. These six women were cast out by their husbands and separated from the Great Bear or Saptarshi constellation to become the Pleiades or Krittika constellation. These tainted wives cast out their unborn children in the forest of reeds on the bank of a river. These foetuses were collected by Svaha, Agni's wife, and merged into a single child with six heads. This child called himself Kartikeya, became the

Six-armed Kartikeya

warrior of the gods, and declared that anyone who disrespects the Krittika would be punished with miscarriage.

In still older Tamil traditions, Kartikeya is known as Murugan who stands on a mountain with his spear and goes down to the plains to battle alongside his mother, the bloodthirsty Kotravai, who in later times came to be known as Chamunda in other parts of India, and eventually as the lion-riding, fortress-protecting battle-goddess Durga. Battle was seen as a sacrifice to the Goddess that led to the creation of kings. There is no connection in the Tamil tradition between Murugan and the Vedic god Agni, or the Puranic god Shiva. Stories such as these reveal how tales of Hindu mythology have changed over space and time, responding to ideas from different geographies and histories.

Six-headed Kartikeya

The six heads of Kartikeya are also a metaphor for the openings or gates (dwaras) of the body-castle, or the nodes (chakras) along the spine that control the internal organs and our moods or for the sense organs (indriyas) that one learns to master through yoga.

Shanmukhi is a conjunction of two Sanskrit words that mean 'six' and 'faces'. A mudra is a 'seal' and usually implies the containing or retention of prana (living energy obtained from the breath). In this pose, the hands are brought over the face in such a way as to block the 'six gates' which are comprised of the two eyes, the two ears, the nose, and the mouth. By 'sealing' these passages, the mind is essentially cut off from sensory perception and is then free to explore its own operation. Though typically performed in the lotus position, this hand mudra can be incorporated into just about any seated or reclined (supine) posture. Obviously, having the nose and mouth covered makes breathing difficult, and as a result, an additional aspect of concentration becomes available in the conscious regulation of the breathing cycle.

40

Mayura-asana
The Peacock Pose

In Hindu mythology, gods are associated with various animals, as they are the vahanas or mounts that the gods ride. Shiva's son Kartikeya rides a peacock. It is interesting that on Mount Kailas there is a peacock whose natural food is the serpent. Shiva has a live serpent coiled around his neck. What do serpents eat? Rats. A rat happens to be the vahana of Ganesha, Shiva's other son. Yet, none of the animals are harmed on Mount Kailas, because, on Mount Kailas, there is no hunger. Thus, through these animals we see that Shiva's abode is a place where one outgrows hunger, fear and desires.

Ganesha is also sometimes shown as riding a peacock, a serpent around his belly. His other mount is the rat. Again, the food chain is depicted. But none of the animals are afraid, as none are hungry. Thus, the heaven of Shiva echoes the biblical concept: the lion shall lie with the lamb!

Hindu mythology has three heavens: those of Indra, Shiva and Vishnu. In the paradise of Indra, full of wish-fulfilling trees (Kalpa-vriksha), wish-fulfilling cows (Kama-dhenu) and wish-fulfilling gems (Chinta-mani), our hungers are indulged. In the paradise of Shiva, we outgrow hunger. In Vishnu's paradise, we take care of other people's hunger. Vishnu, therefore, helps people. Since Indra does not try to satisfy anybody's hunger, hungry creatures, like the asuras, keep attacking him. So, while there is prosperity in Indra's paradise, there is no peace. He is constantly under siege and fighting wars to protect what is 'his'. There is peace in Kailas, but there is no prosperity. However, there is no need for prosperity, as nobody wants anything. In Vishnu's heaven, there is peace and prosperity, for all his needs have been met, and he now works towards satisfying the needs of others.

Vishnu puts a peacock feather in his crown to remind us of how he dances like a peacock among peahens, his beloved, gopis, or milkmaids. The peacock feather, with its eye-shaped mark, is used to ward off the evil eye in many folk practices across India. These eyes were gifted to the peacock by Indra, king of the gods, when he rested in the shade of a peacock's tail in the middle of a war.

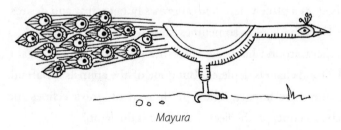

Mayura

A peacock-feather broom is used by Jain monks to clean spaces where they plan to sit, to gently nudge away ants and bugs without harming them, in keeping with their principle of non-violence (ahimsa).

In the Mahayana Buddhist tradition, the goddess of knowledge, Mahamayuri, mother and guardian of the Buddha, is linked with the peacock, perhaps because peacock feathers were commonly used as a writing quill. This inspired images of Saraswati, the Hindu goddess of knowledge, with the peacock, though she is more commonly associated with a swan.

Balance, by definition, is the 'even distribution' of something. When it comes to the practice of asana, we are usually referring to the even distribution of body weight, and this Peacock pose may be the most elegant demonstration of that principle. This pose also addresses a common misconception about what the core muscles are. The term 'core', at least in most people's minds nowadays, has become synonymous with the abdominal muscles (specifically, rectus abdominus – the 'six-pack' muscles), but this is only partially correct. In practical terms, your core is essentially anything that is not your arms and legs, and so the core musculature includes not only your abdominals, but also the majority of your chest and back. The misconception usually leads practitioners to flex in a way that is akin to doing a sit-up when they are asked to activate their 'core', when, in fact, the idea is really to activate all of the associated muscles so as to make the body as rigid as possible. This rigidity offers a platform that can then be 'stacked' on the supporting bone structure. An analogy I frequently make to illustrate this concept is baking a wedding cake. A wedding cake is usually composed of successively smaller cakes that are stacked on top of each other, but if the cake in the middle section isn't baked all the way, everything above it will collapse. The secret (if there is such a thing in asana practice) to success in these postures is learning to properly and completely 'bake the cake'.

41

Gaja-asana
The Elephant Pose

The Puranas state that Shiva, being immortal, wanted no children, but his wife Parvati did. When he refused to give her a child, she created one of her own, using the scrubbings of the perfumed unguents with which she anointed her body. She moulded a doll and breathed life into it. This child did not let Shiva enter her cave. Enraged, Shiva beheaded him, not realizing he was Parvati's son. Parvati was inconsolable in her grief, and in order to resurrect her son, Shiva asked his followers to bring him the head of the first living creature they encountered

Ganesha

in the northern direction. The first animal they encountered happened to an elephant. They cut off its head and brought it back. Shiva placed the head on the child's body, brought him back to life, and named him Gajanan, or the elephant-headed one, the son of Shiva and Shakti, who would also be known as Ganapati, the leader of Shiva's wild companions, the ganas. This is a metaphor for the union of still, immortal spiritual reality, uninterested in children and all things worldly, and the ever-transforming material reality which is engaged in the household and wishes to nurture the future generation in the form of children. Ganesha thus symbolizes the yoga of Shiva and Shakti, the end of disharmony between the mind and matter, spirit and substance.

The elephant is a very important and auspicious animal in Hinduism. It is said that a white-skinned elephant, with three pairs of tusks and seven trunks, emerged from the ocean of milk when it was churned and became the vehicle of Indra, the king of the devas, who rules the skies and releases rains from

dark rain-bearing monsoon clouds. The elephant is associated with royal power. It has no natural enemy in the forest and thus commands great respect. The earliest image of Indra riding an elephant comes from Buddhist iconography found in Bhaja caves near Mumbai, India.

Gaja

Yoga Mythology: 64 Asanas and their Stories

Entrapped elephant-king

The conquest of a violent elephant is a common motif in Hindu and Buddhist stories. Krishna calms the mad elephant Kuvalyapida in Mathura and Buddha calms the drunken elephant sent to kill him.

The sexually aroused bull elephant is the symbol of lust, and the fluid that flows out of its temple is called 'mada' in Sanskrit and gives rise to the word madira, or wine.

The goddess of fortune, Lakshmi, who sits on a lotus flower in the middle of a swamp, is surrounded by elephants that spray water on her; this is symbolic of rain, with the elephants representing rain clouds. Water ensures a bountiful harvest, or a fortune which is embodied by Lakshmi. The elephant's love for water and its association with green vegetation makes it a symbol of fertility and prosperity as well as of power. Lakshmi is venerated by Buddhists, Jains and Hindus alike.

In art, the elephant-king is often shown in a lotus pond, enjoying the pleasures of life, until its foot is captured by a crocodile. The elephant-king then picks up a lotus flower and offers it to Vishnu, who emerges from the clouds and liberates him from the crocodile's death grip by releasing his discus, the Sudarshan chakra. This liberation of the elephant king, or gajendra moksha, is a metaphor for liberation from the material world through devotion.

In Buddhist mythology, particularly in the Jataka tales, the Buddha was born as an elephant who voluntarily gave up his tusks to a greedy hunter at great cost to himself, because he valued the wisdom of detachment more than his tusks. In another tale, the Buddha was born as a prince who gave away his royal rain-cloud-attracting

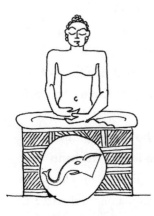

Jina Ajit-nath

white elephant to a neighbouring drought-stricken kingdom. For this act of generosity, the prince was thrown out of the kingdom by his own people, a punishment he accepted with grace, for he valued the wisdom of generosity over holding on to property.

In Jain mythology, the elephant is the emblem of the second of the twenty-four Jinas of this eon, Ajit-nath.

Gaja is the Sanskrit word for 'elephant' and the asana is aptly named for its resemblance to that of an elephant's trunk. Usually done as a precursor to postures like Ashtavakra-asana or Kaundinya-asana, this pose helps develop strength in the arms and abdominals. Another way to think of this posture is something like a half-version of poses like Bhuja Pida-asana (Shoulder Pressure pose), or Tittibha-asana (Flying Insect pose) as they are both arm balances in which the legs are in similar positions behind the shoulders. Another version of this posture is done as a standing forward bend with the arms extended forward, representing the long trunk of an elephant. As has been previously mentioned, there are many interpretations of some asanas, and to argue that one is definitively more 'correct' or more 'traditional' than another is rather trivial, especially considering that most postures practised today are only about a century-old. Some practitioners view this as a point of contention, and somehow this has spurred somewhat of a rivalry between different schools of thought. A simple analogy that often helps put the silliness of this argument into perspective is the idea of asking two different people for directions to the same destination. Where one might offer a path that is more direct and thereby more efficient, the other might offer a path that is more scenic and thus more beautiful to travel along. Who's to say which is more correct? Since both paths ultimately lead to the same destination, the relative 'correctness' of either path is completely subjective.

42

Matsyendra-asana
Matsyendra-nath's Pose

The Nath yogis, or Nath jogis are a special school of yogis that became popular across India about 1000 years ago. They were celibate ascetics, unlike the rishis of Vedic times, and they wandered the earth with just a few possessions such as a blanket, a pair of tongs, a pot, a special earring worn by splitting the ear cartilage (which is why they were called kan-phata or split-eared jogis). They keep chanting 'Alakh Niranjan', the one without attributes (lakshan), and without blemish (anjan) – a name for Shiva. It was they who popularized physical yoga (hatha yoga) with which modern-day yoga is associated. They used the body as an instrument to mystically unite with the divine (samadhi) and attain occult powers (siddhi).

Traditionally, there are nine Naths or Nav Naths who wandered across India, Nepal and South East Asia, spreading their wisdom. They all considered Dattatreya to be their primal guru. Dattatreya is believed to be a form of Shiva on earth. He is depicted with four dogs that represent the four Vedas and a cow that symbolizes the benevolent aspect of the earth-mother. He is also considered the embodiment of the Trimurti: Brahma, Vishnu and Shiva.

Adi guru Dattatreya

Dattatreya is believed to be the first teacher, the teacher of teachers, because he had no formal teacher. Instead his understanding of the world and life came by observing nature and culture: elements, plants, mountains, rivers, animals, birds, insects, men, women, warriors, priests, craftsmen, cooks and courtesans.

Fish overhearing Shiva and Shakti's conversation

The most venerated of the Nath gurus is Matsyendra-nath. Matsyendra-nath was a fish (matsya) who overheard Shiva explaining the secret of yoga to the Goddess. Shiva's words made the fish so wise and powerful, aware and enlightened, that it transformed into a human being, who became a great teacher, admired for his knowledge of mysticism and the occult.

Once, a childless woman came to Matsyendra-nath and asked for a child. He gave her a fistful of ash (raakh) and told her to consume it. However, the woman wasn't sure if a fistful of ash would give her a child, so she threw this ash in a pit in her farm that was full of cow dung (gobar) that was often ignited to make cow dung ash. Nine years later, Matsyendra-nath came to her village again and asked to meet the child he had given her. The woman, still childless, admitted that she had thrown the ash given to her in the pit meant for cow dung and cow dung ash. Matsyendra-nath went to the pit and dug out all the cow dung and cow dung ash, and lo and behold, found a nine-year-old child at the bottom. Matsyendra-nath told the woman that this was supposed to have been her child but, since she had rejected him, the boy now belonged to him. The child came to be known as Gorakh – the one protected by cow dung ash, and who is the protector of cows.

Matsyendra is known as the founder of the Hatha Yoga system, and is generally revered as one of the first teachers of yoga. This asana has many variations that are essentially divided into two categories: the first being the ardha, or 'half', variations like the one pictured here, and the others being the paripurna, or 'full' variations, that involve the inclusion of a half lotus leg and a deeper rotation of the spine. While similar in body positioning to the revolved variations of Marichi-asana (often leaving it overlooked), this posture offers a unique adduction of the lower leg as it crosses the medial line, which in turn provides a stretch of the hips abductors not easy to find in other postures.

43

Goraksha-asana
Gorakh-nath's Pose

Gorakh is the colloquial pronunciation for the Sanskrit word Goraksha, protector of cows, which is slightly different from Gopala, caretaker of cows. The cows here refer to the sense organs that are metaphorically described as constantly grazing on the pastures of stimuli. Goraksha-nath (or Gorakh-nath) is the yogi who protects the sense organs from being carried away by sensory stimuli. Goraksha-nath is famous for rescuing his teacher from a sensory trap, and thus becoming greater than his teacher.

Once upon a time, a princess called Pramila saw the king of gandharvas flying across the sky over her kingdom. From below she could see his genitals and she burst out laughing at the sight. The gandharva king felt so violated that he cursed Pramila that she would live in the middle of a banana grove (Kadali-vana) and no man would be able to enter the forest. If any man tried, he would turn into a woman. Thus, Pramila was trapped in a land of women and wondered how she would ever conceive a child.

The only person who could enter such a forest without losing his masculinity was a siddha yogi, one with occult yogic powers. Matsyendra-nath was one such yogi. Pramila invited him inside, and trapped him with her sensuality and guile and married him; they had a child together. Matsyendra-nath was so happy with her that he forgot his life outside the grove. That is when Goraksha-nath, intending to pull his teacher out of this enchanting kingdom of women, entered the same forest. Goraksha-nath knew that if he entered this forest in his original form, the women would try to seduce him. So he dressed as a woman and pretended to be a dancer and a musician. He kept singing, dancing and playing drums, and gained access to the queen's inner chambers where he saw his teacher. Through cryptic lyrics he told his teacher to open his eyes, realize he was trapped, and escape with his student.

The banana grove, residence of yoginis

When Pramila realized what was happening, she became furious and told Matsyendra-nath to choose between her and his student. To demonstrate his powers, Goraksha-nath picked up Matsyendra-nath's son and killed him, then resurrected him and then killed him again, then

Goraksha-nath

resurrected him again, cut his head off and restored it. By doing so, he showed his guru that, as long as he lived in the kingdom of women, Matsyendra-nath would experience death and suffering; but if he stepped out of it, he would be able to conquer death, by creating life and death at will, and be free from all suffering.

In yoga lore, Matsyendra-nath represents the fierce occult

Flying yogini

Tantric form of yoga, while Goraksha-nath is associated with the milder mystical Vedantic form of yoga. Much of this is oral lore and there are many variations in the tale. Stories such as this are clearly a metaphor, with the forest of women representing both the body and the mundane life of a householder trapped in cupidity. Value was placed on renunciation and fierce

yogic practices that promoted mystical and occult secrets over material power and pleasure.

Shrines dedicated to Goraksha-nath (or Gorakh-nath) are found all over India from Punjab and the Gangetic plains to Bengal, Maharashtra, Andhra Pradesh and Tamil Nadu. The Gorkhas of Nepal trace their spiritual lineage to him.

Once, Goraksha-nath stumbled upon a dry well where he found a man whose hands and feet had been cut off. The man was a prince called Puran, wrongfully accused by his father's junior wife of outraging her modesty. Without bothering to check what had truly happened, the king had ordered that the prince's four limbs be cut off and he be thrown inside a well to die a slow painful death. But Puran survived miraculously, chanting Shiva's name. Goraksha-nath saw the man had no anger or hate towards his father or his stepmother. Realizing the prince was a yogi, Goraksha-nath restored his limbs, named him Chaurangi-nath, the four-armed sage, and accepted him as his student-son.

Another story of Nath yogis speaks of how Gopichand's mother begged her son to give up his wives and his throne and become an ascetic, a follower of Jalandhar-nath, if he wished

Chaurangi-nath

to be immortal. Gopichand's maternal uncle, Bhartrihari, realized that his favourite queen was having an extramarital affair with the elephant keeper as she found her husband sexually inadequate. Heartbroken, he became a mendicant of the Nath order, writing poetry on the

Yoga Mythology: 64 Asanas and their Stories

beauty of the flesh during the waxing phase of the moon and the decay of the flesh in the waning phase of the moon.

Popular in medieval times, these stories tend to be highly misogynistic narratives which portray yogis as seeking the celibate life, and yoginis as corrupting influences, women who derive their power through

Still and grounded yogi

sexual intercourse with yogis, and can turn men into goats through witchcraft. This tension between the yogi and the yogini was very high about 1000 years ago in India. Over time the enchanting female yogini was overshadowed and today we only focus on the male celibate yogi. Tantra's occult side has been reduced in new-age cults to simply a way to get a great orgasm.

This challenging balance posture requires more patience than anything else. While many people are comfortable in the lotus position, it can be especially challenging to find the balance in this posture. It may be helpful to practice while facing a wall at first because otherwise the torso must be bent forward in order to keep the fingertips on the floor when first getting into the asana. This makes finding one's centre of gravity difficult, and the added momentum from the push doesn't help either. Keeping the hands against a wall allows the practitioner to find the proper body orientation needed to eventually balance freely. Once this positioning is well engrained, finding it again while away from the wall becomes much less cumbersome.

———————————

44

Danda-asana
The Staff Pose

The staff is a symbol of royal authority. In the city of Kashi, there is a guardian god called Dandapani, who bears a staff and serves the dog-riding Bhairava, the aspect of Shiva who protects the city. Vishnu, in many depictions, is shown holding the staff, or mace, as he establishes dharma on earth. The Vedic gods Varuna, the god of morality, and Yama, the god of death, who dispassionately determines our fate, are also known to wield the staff. A good king, who bears the royal staff, must establish dharma like Vishnu, be moral like Varuna and detached like Yama.

Yogis are often seen holding a staff in their hand. The staff may contain one bamboo stick or multiple bamboo

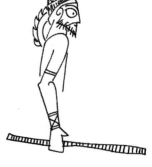

Dandapani

sticks. Each has a very symbolic meaning. For example, three bamboo sticks represent the three gunas, or the three qualities that are found in matter. The eight threads that are tied around them represent the eight steps of yoga. In his bachelor form, Shiva's son Kartikeya is also shown holding a staff – and is called Dandapani, bearer of the staff. The staff is sometimes Y-shaped, so they can rest their arms on it, especially while counting rosary beads as part of name-meditation (nama-japa) to track the name of a deity, which is chanted several hundred or thousand times. Thus, the danda is not just representative of temporal authority but also spiritual authority.

One of the earliest teachers of Shiva's lore was called Lakulesha, he who holds a staff (lakula) in his hand. He is visualized with an erect phallus and holding a staff. The staff thus becomes a metaphor for the erect penis. Western scholars have read the erect phallus of Shiva literally, embarrassing many Hindus, who are upset by this crude, even deliberate, misreading of a powerful symbol. Shiva's linga does not mean Shiva's penis; it means the attribute (linga) of one without any attributes (a-linga). Shiva's phallus is erect but his eyes are shut, which means he is aroused but not through external sensory stimuli, or memories of such stimuli. It is self-raised as an expression of inner tranquillity (anand) born of independence, not dependence, of material

Lakulesha

things. Hence he, and his student, Lakulesha, are hermits, bearing the staff. It is a visual reminder of semen whose movement is reversed up the spine to the head, rather than spilling into a womb, described in Tantra as urdhva-retas. This gives occult powers to the yogi.

This variation of the posture (technically called Yoga Danda-asana) is practised seated, with one leg in an extreme external rotation and the foot tucked under the pit of the arm. The symbolism of this asana is credited to the ascetic devotees of Shiva who use rigid wooden staffs under the arm in a technique employed to control the flow of the breath. One hand is tucked under the rotated leg while the other hand is extended forward and held in the gesture of jnana mudra, the seal of knowledge. Another, probably more widely recognized, version of this asana is known as Chaturanga Danda-asana (Four-limbed Staff pose) as it comes up quite frequently in sequences such as the Surya Namaskar. It generally requires the practitioner to hold the body rigid above the ground while the feet and hands support the body's weight (similar to the bottom portion of a push-up exercise). Yet another version of the Danda-asana calls for the practitioner to be seated with the legs together and extended forward while the torso and head are in a perpendicular alignment with the ground.

———————————

Vishnu

Vishnu is the preserver of culture. He is associated with several avatars; from his heaven, Vaikuntha, which is located in the middle of the ocean of milk, he descends to earth from time to time, taking various forms, to help humans discover wisdom. His most popular avatars are Ram, the king of Ayodhya and the protagonist of the epic Ramayana, and Krishna, the kingmaker in the epic Mahabharata.

An avatar is not a superhero. While a superhero is an ordinary man who becomes extraordinary, like a Greek hero who is allowed to sit with Olympian gods, an avatar is the finite mortal form

Narayana, the sleeping Vishnu

Lakshmi, wealth

of the infinite immortal divine. Unlike a prophet or messiah, an avatar is not a saviour, because in Hindu mythology humans are not 'fallen'; they are caught in the wheel of cause and effect, of birth and death, and being unable to cope with it, they seek meaning. They suffer because they don't understand their role in the world or their purpose in life. Engagement with Vishnu grants them wisdom and a world view that results in peace, happiness and prosperity. Vishnu establishes dharma.

In Buddhism, dhamma (the Pali word for dharma) means following the path of the Buddha. In Jainism, dharma means movement, an eternal principle of the cosmos. In Hinduism, dharma means being true to one's nature. For the elements, dharma is following the laws of physics. For

Matsya nyaya

animals, it is following the law of the jungle, known in Sanskrit as matsya nyaya (fish justice): the big eat the small to survive. For humans, dharma is overcoming the law of the jungle in order to establish civilization: the big help the small. To achieve this, Vishnu

lives like a householder. However, unlike Brahma, he neither yearns for, nor is attached to wealth, power, property, status, his household or to the world at large, much like the hermit Shiva. This makes Vishnu the hermit-householder, living as a householder, but thinking like a hermit. While Brahma and his children, the devas and the asuras for instance, engage for the benefit of the self, Vishnu engages for the benefit of the other,

As long as Vishnu is sleeping on the coils of a multi-headed serpent, the world does not exist; it comes into being when he awakens. He then takes various avatars, beginning with the fish and ending with the horse-riding warrior, before he goes back to sleep once again on the ocean of milk, and the world ceases to be. Unlike Shiva, who smears himself with ash and wears animal hide, Vishnu anoints himself with perfumes and sandal paste, decorates himself with fragrant flowers and wears bright silk fabrics, indicating his comfort with culture. He enjoys life. He is a connoisseur of the arts. He fights but does not hate. He loves but does not control. He smiles for he can see how humans delude themselves.

Vishnu is the beloved of Lakshmi, the goddess of fortune. While everyone wants fortune, fortune chases Vishnu, but he is not interested in possessing her or controlling her. He attracts her as he engages with culture without being possessive about anything. Humans seek to possess because they don't know who they are and confuse who they are with what they possess. Vishnu does not need wealth or status to establish who he is in society. He is attached to

Vishnu on Garuda

nothing but accepts his responsibilities that come to him with birth. Thus, as Ram he is king because he is the eldest son in the royal family; it is an obligation, not ambition. As Krishna, he is a cowherd and does not consider serving as a charioteer demeaning.

Many scholars have compared the relationship between the world-affirming Vishnu and the world-rejecting Shiva to the Greek gods Apollo and Dionysus. Apollo and Vishnu are associated with cultural order while Dionysus and Shiva are seen as disrupters who challenge the rules. But the fundamental difference between Greek and Hindu mythology has to do with the belief in rebirth. Shiva is located outside the wheel of rebirth. So is Vishnu, but he does step into the wheel of rebirth as a mortal avatar – sometimes the rule-following august Ram, and sometimes the rule-breaking romantic Krishna.

45

Ananta-asana
Ananta's Pose

Vishnu is visualized in art as reclining or seated on the coils of Adi Ananta Sesha, the cosmic serpent with a thousand hoods who floats on the ocean of milk. Adi means primal, ananta means infinite and sesha means residue. The cosmic serpent, thus, embodies time that has neither beginning nor end, and is coiled to create the couch of Vishnu. Ananta is imagined as the cradle of time that rocks the cosmic being when nothing exists.

When Vishnu sleeps, the world ceases to exist; when Vishnu wakes up, the world comes into being. Thus, in the Hindu world view, the world is not the creation of

Adi Ananta Shesha

objective reality but the creation of
subjective reality. With the waking
up of the mind, the world outside is
experienced within.

Ananta accompanies Vishnu when
he descends to earth: as Lakshman,
his younger brother, when Vishnu
descends as Ram, the king of
Ayodhya; and as his cousin Balaram,
the farmer, when Vishnu descends as
Krishna, the cowherd.

*Vishnu sleeping
on Ananta*

In many versions of the tale, Ananta coils around Mount
Meru and allows himself to be used as a churning rope by the
devas and the asuras who churn the ocean of milk. From this

Ananta as churning rope

enterprise emerge various
treasures of the world that
grant power, prosperity,
pleasure and even wisdom.
The churning was so
vigorous that Ananta spat
out a terrifying poison that
could only be consumed
by Shiva, thanks to his
yogic powers. It served as a reminder that all good things
are accompanied by the bad. Unless one can handle the bad
through yoga, one cannot enjoy the good.

Shiva uses Ananta as the cosmic bowstring, with Meru as
the shaft of his bow, to destroy, with a single arrow, the three

worlds inhabited by the asuras who have abandoned Vedic wisdom. Thus, the same serpent and the same mountain used to churn the ocean for treasures, when Vedic wisdom waxes, transform into a weapon of destruction, when Vedic wisdom wanes.

It is also said that the earth rests on the hood of Ananta Sesha; when he moves, earthquakes happen.

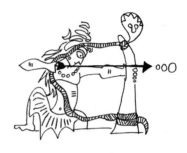

Ananta as Shiva's bowstring

Multi-headed serpents are a recurring motif in Hindu, Buddhist and Jain mythology and probably originated long ago as symbol of all things mysterious, from fertility to occult powers.

Ananta-asana is named for Vishnu's giant serpent, upon which Vishnu assumes a carefree position of relaxation even as he maintains the steady rhythm of the cosmos. This posture, though seemingly easy, requires a fair amount of concentration to prevent falling. Like balancing on a log floating on water, one must pay careful attention to the vertical positioning of the extended leg in order to prevent 'rolling out' of this pose. For practitioners who struggle to reach the toe in this particular range of motion, the practice of this asana can be modified by looping a belt or strap around the extended foot for a better sense of connection and improved stability.

———

46

Garuda-asana
The Eagle Pose

Vishnu reclines on a serpent, but flies around the world on an eagle (some say a kite or falcon). This is Garuda, king of the birds. He displays integrity because he held the pot (kumbha) of the nectar of immortality (amrita) in his beak but did not sip from it, as it did not belong to him.

Garuda's mother, Vinata, was enslaved by her sister Kadru and Kadru's children, the serpents (nagas). The serpents demanded the pot of nectar for her freedom. Garuda managed to enter the paradise of Indra, fight Indra and the devas, and fetch the nectar of

Nagas in Garuda's talons

immortality. He then brought it down to the serpent realm, without drinking even a drop of it. This impressed the gods so much that Vishnu made Garuda his vehicle and his symbol, that is found on the flag (dhvaja) that accompanies Vishnu wherever he goes. Many Hindu gods have flags that display their symbols. Shiva's flag, for example, has the symbol of the bull.

It is significant that Vishnu sleeps on a serpent and rides the eagle. Serpents and eagles are natural enemies; the serpent eats the bird's eggs and the eagle hunts the serpent. However, Vishnu works with both predator and prey, which is why he is the preserver. He knows the value of the serpent and the eagle and does not favour one over the other, for he knows each plays an important role in the cosmos. Garuda evokes the bird's-eye view, or the strategic gaze of humanity, and the serpent embodies the worm's-eye view, or the tactical view of

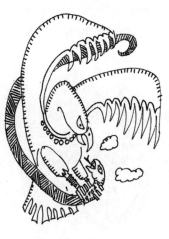

Garuda and serpent

humans. Thus, Vishnu has both a wide vision as well as the focused vision of the world, which makes him the great observer and guardian of the world.

In the Ramayana, Garuda swoops down to free Ram from the venomous coils of serpents shot from the arrows of Meghnad. In the Mahabharata, Krishna rides into battle on Garuda to defeat the asuras

Naraka and Bana. Riding Garuda, Krishna also defeats Indra, king of the devas. In art, Garuda is increasingly visualized less as an eagle and more as a parrot, to show Vishnu and Krishna's close association with Kama, the god of love.

In Jain mythology, the falcon is the symbol of the fourteenth Jina of this eon, Ananta-nath. According to the Jatakas the Buddha-to-be was born as Sakka, king of the thirty-three devas, who live atop Mount Meru. When attacked by the asuras, who live at the base of the mountain, the devas, Sakka included, ran towards the sky. But when Sakka realized that his flying chariot would smash into an eagle's nest and kill the baby eagles, he turned around. He had no choice then but to face the marauding asuras. His decision,

Jina Ananta-nath

born out of compassion, motivated the devas to also turn around and rally behind Sakka. In the battle that followed, the asuras were defeated and a truce was declared. The asura princess Suja married Sakka.

Stories of Garuda spread to South East Asia over 1000 years ago via sea-faring merchants, and are still very popular. The national airline of Indonesia, a Muslim-dominated country, is called Garuda Indonesia, a sign of the country's cultural roots.

People are often surprised to learn that this asana is not intended to be a representation of an eagle (even though it is often referred to simply as the Eagle pose). This posture actually depicts the hero Ram, wrapped and bound by snakes on the battlefield of Lanka during an engagement with Ravana's son, Meghnad (also known as Indrajit). Garuda flies down from on high and eats the snakes, freeing Ram from his bonds and allowing him to return to the battle against his wife's captor. This is yet another example of why avoiding generic labels like 'Eagle pose' is so important. Knowing the story behind the name gives depth to the practice and inspires one to seek further understanding of its origins.

47

Mala-asana
The Garland Pose

Hindu gods are usually associated with garlands. While Shiva's garland is a string of rudraksh beads, which are, essentially, seeds of the rudraksh plant, Vishnu's garland is made of leaves and flowers. The difference in their respective garlands reveals how Shiva's hermit form and his gradual transformation into a householder by the Goddess is the seed that gives rise to the enlightened hermit-householder embodied in Vishnu. The goddess Kali wears a garland of male human heads around her neck. This is known as munda-mala, a reminder that nature ultimately claims the life of all organisms and does not consider anyone special. Male heads symbolize the human ego that must be crushed for mankind to appreciate the true nature of the Goddess, and the world.

Vishnu is called Vanamali, he who drapes forest flowers around his neck. He is also known as Vaijayanti, he who wears the victory garland around his neck. These garlands are typically made of fragrant, colourful, dew-drenched, nectar-rich flowers that attract bees and butterflies. These indicate association with life and participation in the world. They also link Vishnu to Kama, the god of love, whom Shiva reduces to ash with a glance of his

Devi with a garland of human heads

third eye. While Kama drives humans mad with lust, like bees driven to flowers, Vishnu expands the mind so that pleasure is obtained not by taking for the self, but by giving to the other.

If the seeds around Shiva's neck represent potential, then Vishnu represents the realization of the potential in the form of leaves and flowers, in terms of fragrance, colour and sweetness. Vishnu adorns himself and makes himself attractive, unlike

Vishnu with a garland of flowers and leaves from the forest

Shiva, who covers his body with ash and makes himself unappealing and unattractive to the world so that he can withdraw and live in isolation. Their complementary personalities complete the picture of divinity.

In mythological stories, we learn of women garlanding men whom they wish to

Shiva with a garland of rudraksh seeds

marry. Garlands are also offered to guests on their arrival. In the Ramayana, a celestial garland falls from the sky and startles Indumati, who dies instantly, breaking the heart of her husband, Aja, who is the grandfather of Ram. In the Mahabharata, Amba goes around the world, garland in hand, looking for a man who will avenge her humiliation.

According to folklore, a garland around a wise man's neck never withers but that around a fool's neck does, as the wise man never gets agitated while the fool does. Malini is the name of a yogini who makes garlands during the day but practices occult arts secretly at night.

Jain stories inform us that a garland is one of the auspicious objects that appear in the dreams of women who will be mothers of great kings, warriors and hermits.

Mala is the Sanskrit word for 'garland' and it often refers to a collection of beads on a string. For example, the japa mala is a common fixture used in the practice of meditation or devotional prayer, and it generally consists of 108 beads (or seeds) which are counted in succession as the mantras are chanted. From a deep squat and with the feet together, the torso is folded forward and the arms are wrapped around the fronts of the legs. The completion of the garland is accomplished by bringing the fingers to touch or by binding the hands together in a bandha ('bind') at one's back. Practitioners often work towards developing this asana by creating a connection between the hands with the use of a belt or strap.

48

Chakra-asana
The Wheel Pose

Vishnu is visualized as a four-armed god. He holds in his hands a conch shell trumpet (shankh), a wheel weapon (chakra), a mace (gada) and a lotus flower (padma). As bearer of the chakra he is called Chakrapani. In many temples, Vishnu's chakra is worshipped as a deity in his own right, known as Chakra-purusha.

Vishnu's wheel, known as Sudarshan chakra, is similar to a boomerang: once it is released, it severs enemies' necks and then returns to Vishnu's hand. With the chakra, Vishnu beheaded the demon, Rahu, an asura who drank the nectar of immortality, or amrita. The head which contained the amrita became Rahu, or the demon of the eclipse, and the remaining wriggling tail became the comet Ketu, the embodiment of restlessness.

The spoked wheel of a chariot is also called a chakra. When Shiva rode into battle against the three worlds controlled by asuras, his chariot was the earth whose wheels were made of the sun and the moon. A chakra of fire forms around Shiva when he does the tandava dance.

Vishnu holding his chakra

The chakra represents space in Indic mythology, be it Buddhist, Jain or Hindu. The centre of the wheel represents Mount Meru, the centre of the sacred world as per all Indic mythologies, from where stretch the rivers that reach the periphery, which is the ocean. It is a metaphor for the spine with the rivers representing the channels (nadis) that connect the senses to the brain. The king who rules the world is called Chakravarti, as his power extends to the horizon which is circular in shape like a wheel. Metaphorically, he is intellect, master of our mind.

The chakra also represents the cyclical nature of time. In Hindu mythology, time repeats itself and, in every age, as

the wheel of time moves, the eras change, from childhood (Krita-yuga) to youth (Treta-yuga) to maturity (Dwapar-yuga) and finally senility (Kali-yuga), which is followed by the death of the cosmos or Pralaya. After this there is a rebirth and the cycle repeats itself. In Jain mythology, as the wheel turns, things

Spoked wheel

The seven chakras

get better (sushama) and then they get worse (dushama), again and again. This cyclical nature of time means that everything in this world is repeated. There is nothing unique. Every time the world takes new shape, Vishnu descends in his various avatars, as Ram, the king, and as Krishna, the cowherd, to solve problems. Unlike Christian mythology, where the world is moving towards Judgement Day (Qayamat in Islam), Hindu mythology sees the world moving towards death and rebirth constantly, thus experiencing a very different kind of world view.

The chakra, in Tantric traditions, represents the nodes of the spine that control the various organs of the body.

Chakra	Rainbow Colour	Frontal Location	Spinal Location	Gland	Metaphor
Muladhara	Red	Anus	Coccyx	Adrenaline	Fear
Svadhishtana	Orange	Genitals	Sacrum	Gonads	Desire
Manipura	Yellow	Navel	Lumbar	Pancreas	Hunger
Anahata	Green	Heart	Thoracic	Thymus	Feeling
Vishuddha	Blue	Throat	Cervical	Thyroid	Communication
Ajna	Indigo	Forehead	Lower brain	Pituitary	Insight
Sahashrara	Violet	Crown	Frontal brain	Pineal	Wisdom

This dynamic series of movements represents the turning of a wheel, or the whirling of Vishnu's discus, the Sudarshan chakra. This sequence is usually initiated from a fully reclined position (lying on the back). As the legs come up over the hips, the hands move, bringing the fingertips to the shoulders. As the legs swing over, the hands press firmly into the ground, raising the hips and allowing clearance for the head. Once the feet are firmly grounded, one continues pressing into the hands until the arms are straight, and the practitioner ultimately ends up in the Downward-facing Dog pose (Adhomukha Svanana-asana). In Western adaptations of asana practice, this pose has gotten confused with the Urdhva Dhanura-asana (Upward Bow pose), or simply called the Wheel pose. However, much like the Surya Namaskar, this asana is a rolling series of movements that represent the motion of a wheel.

49

Bala-asana
The Child Pose

One day, the sage Markandeya had a vision about how the world would come to an end. Just as human beings die, the world also experiences death. This is called Pralaya, when all the mountains, forests, lands and rivers get submerged under the sea, where they dissolve into the waters. This frightening sight where even the stars and the planets are consumed by the sea was witnessed by Markandeya. As the vision continued, the sage saw a banyan leaf, cradled by the waves of the waters of doom. On this banyan leaf was a child, a baby sucking its toe. This was Vishnu as an infant. Markandeya was reassured that what he had seen as the terrifying end of the world was just an event in the lifecycle of the cosmos. Death would be followed by rebirth, not only for all living creatures, but the world itself. The gurgling happy child represented how the divine considers even the greatest

Baby Krishna on a leaf

of catastrophes and calamities as just one event in the infinite flow of events that take place in the universe.

The infant then breathed in deeply and Markandeya was sucked into his body. Within it, he saw the whole world reorganize and restructure anew, with the celestial regions above, the earth below and beneath that, the realms of serpents and asuras. He realized that everything that is broken down is eventually put together by the gods. The world goes through cyclical phases of creation and destruction. He also realized that everything is contained within and without divinity. Thus, through the child form, Vishnu explained the nature of the world (according to Hinduism) to Markandeya, and Markandeya shared it with the rest of the world. In Hindu mythology, God often appears in the form of a child, not only to embody childlike innocence, but also to enable devotees to experience him through the mode of parental affection. Emotions become the highway through which the divine can be experienced and one of the emotions is that of parental affection.

The cosmic child

Although Vishnu is visualized as a baby when he descends on earth as Ram and Krishna, there are some traditions that see Shiva as a baby too. In this form, he calms the wild and angry goddess Kali by appealing to her maternal instinct. Shiva's children, Ganesha and Kartikeya (Murugan) are also visualized as children to evoke parental affection in devotees.

Krishna, the child

In the Puranas, there are even sages such as the four Sanat-kumars who look like children, to remind us of their innocent and pure nature.

In the Bhagavata Purana, there are many stories of Krishna in his childhood. How he frightens and fights demons, delights his mother with his love for butter and shows her the whole world in his mouth.

Perhaps the simplest and most 'grounding' of asanas, the child pose is a very calming position and is accessible to almost any practitioner. This posture is usually done in one of two variations. The first entails keeping the knees together and allowing the torso to drape over the legs. This particular variation offers a little more rounding of the lower back. The second variation consists of bringing the knees apart just wide enough so that the torso can settle between the thighs. This variation offers a slightly deeper stretch through the hips, but also allows for a straighter spine to accommodate those with lower-back pain.

50

Matsya-asana
The Fish Pose

Matsya nyaya, or fish justice, is a very important concept in Hindu mythology. It is the Sanskrit equivalent of the English phrase, 'law of the jungle'. In the sea, the big fish eat the small fish and that is perfectly acceptable. However, in the human world, such behaviour, where the strong exploit the weak, is considered unacceptable. In the human world, the world of culture, the strong are expected to take care of the weak. This is a reversal of matsya nyaya. This reversal is dharma. When human beings behave like animals and exploit the weak, they follow adharma.

Matsya Nyaya

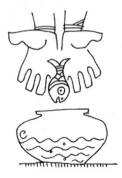

Fish in a pot

In Vishnu's first avatar, he takes the form of a small fish and asks the first human being, Manu, to protect him from the large fish. Manu takes the small fish and puts him in a pot and protects him from the large fish. The next day, however, the small fish has grown and needs a bigger pot. Subsequently, larger and larger pots are required to house the fish. Eventually, the fish becomes so big that it has to be put into a river from where it swims to the sea, promising that, one day, he will come back to rescue Manu.

One day, it rains so heavily that the earth begins to get submerged in water. Manu realizes that the world is coming to an end; he doesn't know what to do. Suddenly, the big fish appears on the horizon and tells him to take all that matters – the best seeds, all the plants, all the animals, the knowledge of the Vedas – and board a ship that will be towed to safety by the fish, which is none other than Vishnu himself.

Vishnu thus rescues Manu in the same way that Manu rescued him. When Manu was strong, he protected the weak fish, and when Manu was weak, he was rescued by the strong fish. The strong must always help the weak, for by helping the weak, they make them strong, so that they, in turn, can help others in

Matsya pulling Manu's Ship

Fish Jataka

need. This is considered the hallmark of civilization. This is dharma, instituted and maintained by Vishnu.

In the Jatakas, the Buddha-to-be is born as a fish and he helps other fish escape the fisherman's net and in times of drought, when the fish are trapped in mud and are at the mercy of crows, he uses his merits to make it rain so that the fish can escape.

In Jain art, the fish is the symbol of Ara-nath, the eighteenth Jina of the current eon. Before he became the Jina, he was also a Chakravarti (ruler of a vast empire) and a Kama-deva (most desired man).

Jina Ara-nath

With the large display of the ribs and the angular shape of the legs folded into Padma-asana, this pose closely resembles the body of a fish. Support for the upper body comes from the arm bones, and the contact between the hands and feet allows one to gradually pull the body into a deeper arch. However, given that the neck is a fragile part of the body, one should always be mindful not to rest one's entire weight on the head, nor should one ever turn their head from side-to-side while any additional load is being borne by the cervical spine.

———————

51

Nava-asana
The Boat Pose

We have all heard of Noah's Ark in the Bible. A similar story exists in Hindu mythology, of how Manu carried the sacred Vedas along with plants and animals and the seven primal sages in a boat through the waters of Pralaya, and found refuge atop Mount Meru.

In the Ramayana, Ram travels by boat across the river that separates his kingdom of Ayodhya from the forest where he is to be exiled for fourteen years. In the Mahabharata, a fisherwoman called Satyavati ferries a sage called Parasara across a river by boat. The sage falls in love with her and together they have a child. Because of his magical powers, the child is conceived and

Ship with Manu and the seven sages

delivered before the boat reaches the other bank. The child grows up instantly and goes to live on an island in the middle of the river. This child later comes to be known as Vyasa, the great compiler of the Vedas.

Satyavati and Parasara

While many people associate Hinduism, like Buddhism, with austerity and meditation, Hinduism also values the household world, the world of love, romance and responsibilities. For instance, Krishna is a romantic god who goes on boat rides in Vrinda-vana with his beloveds, and in Dwarka with his eight queens. Thus, romance and luxury are integral to Krishna worship. They evoke the mood of love. The

Krishna and Radha on a boat

boat is also a symbol of survival on the stormy oceans of the material world, through devotion to Krishna. In Krishna temples, on moonlit nights, the images of Krishna and his consorts are taken on boat rides for his pleasure.

In Jataka tales that describe the previous lives of the Buddha, we learn of the prince Mahajanaka who was travelling on a boat to Suvarnabhumi (South East Asia) to seek his fortune. However, the boat got caught in a storm. A shipwreck was inevitable. While everyone else panicked, he remained calm, and ate a vast meal so that he could survive the days of starvation that he anticipated post the shipwreck. While his fellow sailors drowned, he held on to

Mahajanaka

the mast of the boat so that he could stay afloat. After seven days, he was recognized as the future Buddha and rescued by Manimeghalai, the goddess of the sea, and brought to shore.

This challenging asana is designed to strengthen the abdominal muscles and hip flexors. The shape of the posture represents the hull of a ship with the arms representing the water line as it sails. There are many variations of this posture, and many modifications can be done to make it more accessible. One such modification is to bend the knees so that the shins are parallel to the floor. When the legs are straight, the abdominals and hip flexors have to fight against the hamstrings to maintain the posture, but bending the knees relieves the tension in the back of the legs and can make the posture considerably less strenuous.

52

Kurma-asana
The Turtle Pose

The Jatakas tell us that in one of his previous lives, the Buddha was a turtle who witnessed a shipwreck. He rescued the sailors by letting them take refuge on his back, and conveying them to a nearby island. The sailors were happy to be alive, but they were also hungry. They decided to eat the turtle who had saved them. Being a Bodhisattva, the turtle did not mind and in his infinite compassion allowed himself to be eaten.

For Jains, the turtle is the symbol of Muni-Suvrat or simply Suvrat, the Jina who lived in the time of Ram. For Hindus, the turtle is the

Buddha-to-be as a turtle

mount of the river Yamuna, and a sign of the river's sluggish flow – compared to the river Ganga's, whose goddess rides a dolphin. Images of these two river goddesses riding their respective mounts adorn the gates of many temples.

Tortoise is called Kashyapa in Sanskrit; perhaps an allusion to Rishi Kashyapa, the father of devas and asuras, on account of his patience with his quarrelling sons. The turtle is seen as the symbol of longevity and often considered the base of the earth.

The most important turtle icon is of Vishnu himself. This story is found not just in India but in many countries of South East Asia such as Thailand and Cambodia which once traded with sea-merchants from India. It involves two sets of Brahma's warring descendants: the devas, who live above the sky, and the asuras, who live below the earth.

A time came when the devas did not find happiness and splendour in anything, so they went to their father, Brahma, who said that all the things that could make their lives wonderful were dissolved in the ocean of milk. They had to be churned out. The devas did not know how to churn the

Vishnu's kurma avatar

ocean and so approached Vishnu who asked Garuda to carry Mount Meru to the middle of the sea so that it could serve as a churning rod and he asked Ananta, his serpent (Vasuki, king of serpents in other retellings), to coil around the mountain and serve as churning rope. Vishnu himself took the form of a turtle, or kurma, and kept this cosmic churn afloat on his back. On Vishnu's advice, the asuras were made the counterforce of the churn. Left to themselves, the warring half-brothers would have played tug-of-war with Sesha. But instead, following Vishnu's instructions, the devas pulled when the asuras paused, and the asuras pulled when the devas paused. Thus the ocean of milk was churned and great treasures emerged that made life joyful, all thanks to Vishnu, in his turtle avatar.

In Shiva temples, one always finds the image of a turtle for it represents the yogi who can easily withdraw from the world as a turtle retracts its limbs into its shell.

Jina Suvrat

The shape of this asana represents the body of a turtle and is dedicated to the second avatar of Vishnu, Kurma. This posture requires a lot of flexibility in the hamstrings and proper consideration with regard to placement of the shoulders. Standing postures such as Prasarita Padottana-asana or the standing variation of Tittibha-asana are excellent preparations for this particular asana. Forcing the legs to straighten while they rest on top of the shoulders can lead to lasting injuries, and practitioners should work through the progressions of this pose carefully. Placing blocks under the ankles to help support the weight of the legs is a useful modification when developing hamstring flexibility for this asana. Again, one should never sacrifice one's well-being for the sake of practising a yoga pose. One of the cornerstones of yoga is ahimsa (non-violence), which is usually interpreted as doing no harm to others, but in truth, its meaning could (and should) be interpreted as doing no harm to anyone, including ourselves.

53

Varaha-asana
The Boar Pose

The Puranas narrate the story of an asura who dragged the earth under the sea while she cried out for help. At that moment, a boar emerged from the nostrils of Brahma, plunged into the sea, battled the asura and, after gorging him to death, lifted the earth with its snout and raised her to the surface of the sea. As the boar arose, he held the earth close. That intimate embrace resulted in the earth folding upon herself to create mountains and valleys. The tusks plunged into the earth and impregnated her. Thus, all plants came into being. This magnificent boar is the Varaha, an avatar of Vishnu.

Varaha

In Ancient India, the wild boar avatar of Vishnu was the symbol of virility and royalty. However, over time these animal forms of Vishnu were overshadowed by his more human forms such as Ram and Krishna.

The varaha or wild boar is the symbol of the Tirthankara Vimal-nath in Jain mythology. It is also the mount

Varahi

of the guardian goddess Marichi, who in Chinese Mahayana Buddhism is associated with the sun. In some biographies, the Buddha died as a result of food poisoning; his last meal was wild boar meat, which he ate, even though he shunned meat, out of compassion for the man offering the meal. Others refute this claim and insist his last meal was wild mushrooms.

Boar-riding Marichi, Buddhist goddess of dawn

Buddhist symbol of craving

In Buddhist art, a pig is considered the symbol of attraction, and is often visualized along with a rooster, the symbol of attachment, and a snake, the symbol of revulsion, in the wheel of life. These three are the indicators of craving that bring misery into our lives.

In Tantra, one of the most powerful goddesses associated with fertility and power is Varahi, the sow goddess. In Karnataka, in the Tulu-nadu region, locals worship a forest-spirit or bhuta known as Panjurli who is visualized either with the face of a wild boar or riding a wild boar. He can protect fields from being devastated by wild boars. In local mythology, humans have access to two worlds – the wild forest (aranya-loka) and the domesticated field (gramya-loka). But the shaman–priest–king has access to the bhuta-loka as well and asks the various bhutas to protect the field from creatures of the forest and ensure peace and prosperity.

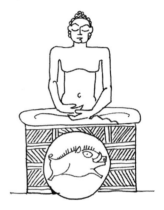

Jina Vimal-nath

Varaha is the Sanskrit word for a 'wild boar'. In this posture, the raised points of the elbows represent the tusks of a boar. Both variations of this pose offer a deep squat with the feet together; however, one provides a deep stretch through the back of the lower legs (with the heels down on the ground) while the heels-raised variation provides a more challenging balance component.

———————————

54

Simha-asana
The Lion Pose

The lion is the mount of the goddess Durga as she rides into battle. The lion, the alpha predator in the jungle, is associated with kingship across the world, even in lands where lions do not roam, such as faraway China and Singapore. The king's throne in India was called the simhasana or the lion-throne. The main entrance of a royal palace is often called simhadwara or the lion-gate.

It is said that Vishnu once took the form of a strange creature, half lion and half human, to destroy an asura who could not be defeated by a human or an animal. Thus, Vishnu took a composite form – Narasimha – which was neither this nor that. The Narasimha form of

Narasimha

275

Vishnu embodies the queer space, which belongs neither here or there. This form was taken to humble a king who thought he was master of all categories, and did not believe in the possibility of failure. In nature there are no categories; that's a human construct. As Narasimha, the divine shatters these human constructs.

Once, a cow asked a king to protect him from a lion. When the king tried to stop the lion, the beast asked, 'If you don't let

The lion and the deer

me eat the cow, how will I survive? The cow is my natural food.' So, the king asked the lion to eat deer. The lion argued that the king had hunted down all the deer and there were none left in the forest, leaving him no choice but to come to the pastures and prey on the cow. The king then offered his own body instead of the cow. The lion laughed, saying that the king's body would feed him only for a day. What about the next day and the day after that? The story draws attention to the tension between domesticated spaces and wild spaces. As humans create pastures and encroach on the forest, the forest creatures, embodied in the lion, wonder where they should go. This creates tension between humans and animals, which is ever-prevalent today and is a recurring theme in Hindu mythology. The king must follow dharma and protect the cow, but it is also an ethical dilemma, a dharma-sankat – because in protecting the cow he is causing the lion to starve and is also responsible for the other creatures that the lion will kill. The king who sits on the throne must decide if he wants to be the alpha predator or the protector of the weak.

In Jain mythology, the twenty-fourth Jina of this eon, Mahavira, has a lion as his symbol. In the Jatakas, the Buddha-to-be is born as a lion and has many good as well as bad adventures with a fox. In one story, the fox gets the lion to attack the king's horses, as a result of which the lion is shot by the royal archers. In another, the fox thinks he is as good as a lion, tries to hunt an elephant, and gets killed. In a third story, the lion and the fox become friends and live together, but their families quarrel, forcing the two to separate.

Jina Mahavira

Similar to the Upward-facing Dog pose (Urdhvamukha Svana-asana), this pose entails folding the legs into Padma-asana while pressing into the hands to lift the chest. Additionally, the face gets some interesting attention in this posture as the gaze is brought to the tip of the nose and the tongue is fully extended out towards the chin. In Sanskrit, simha means 'lion', but can also be translated as 'hero' or 'eminent person'.

55

Ganda Bherunda-asana
Ganda Bherunda's Pose

Once upon a time, an asura obtained from Brahma a boon – he could not be killed during the day or at night, neither inside nor outside a dwelling, by neither human nor animal. To destroy him, Vishnu took the form of the man–lion Narasimha, who is neither human nor animal. He caught hold of the asura and dragged him to the threshold of his home, which was neither inside or outside the dwelling, at twilight, which is neither day or night, ripped open his chest and killed him.

But when Narasimha consumed the asura's blood he was filled with blood lust and lost all memory of his divine state. To control him, Shiva had to take the form of Sharabha, an eight-legged lion with a serpent's tail. When Shiva, in this form, overpowered Vishnu in his Narasimha avatar, he became arrogant and started believing himself to be the most

powerful creature in the world. To rid
him of his vanity, Vishnu appeared
before Shiva in the form of the Ganda
Bherunda, a two-headed eagle so
enormous that it can catch elephants in
its four claws. This terrifying pose was
taken by Vishnu to overpower Shiva.

Ganda Bherunda

These stories come from sectarian
Hindu traditions. Broadly, Hindu
traditions can be divided into Shiva
worshipers and Vishnu worshipers.
This rivalry led to stories where each group tried to show
that their deity was greater. Eventually, everyone agreed that
Vishnu and Shiva are the same: they represent two aspects of
the same divinity – Shiva, the hermit side of the divine and
Vishnu, the householder form of the divine.

While in Greek mythology, monsters like the Chimera
and the Sphinx represent chaos and have to be destroyed by

Sharabha

heroes, in Hindu mythology, monsters are
forms taken by gods to show humans the
limits of human imagination. What does
not exist in human reality exists in the
imagination of God.

In Japanese Buddhist mythology, we
learn the story of the two-headed bird
called Gumyocho that lived in India. One
head was called Karuda and the other was
called Upakaruda. The two heads had

opposite personalities. When one woke up, the other slept, when one wanted to play, the other wanted to rest. One day, Karuda ate tasty fruits while Upakaruda was sleeping. When Upakaruda woke up, he saw that Karuda had eaten all the fruits and their shared stomach was full. Enraged because he could not taste the fruit himself, he ate poisonous fruit to make Karuda sick, not realizing that the poison in the shared stomach would kill him too. Before dying, he realized the value of interconnectedness which is why he was reborn in Sukhavati, the Pure Land paradise of Amitabha Buddha.

This pose is one of the most challenging postures there is. Many variations of this asana appear in different styles of the practice, such as the chin-stand variation pictured here. A 'full' expression of the asana involves an incredibly deep backbend with the feet brought all the way to the floor outside the face. The arms are then placed over the feet and the hands are tucked under the chin with the fingers interlaced. This pose serves as a reminder that not all postures are meant for all bodies and attaching an emotional value to 'achieving' a posture in yoga is often a short path to long-term suffering. Postures like this one must be practised responsibly, and only under the guidance of qualified teachers.

56

Trivikrama-asana
Trivikrama's Pose

Once upon a time there was an asura, who was so powerful that he could not be defeated in war. He claimed mastery over the three worlds: the earth, the atmosphere and the sky. He became so powerful and arrogant that he offered to grant people whatever they desired in the world. So, Vishnu took the form of a dwarf and asked the asura for three paces of land. 'Is that all?' said the asura, looking at the dwarf's short stature. 'Yes,' said the dwarf. As soon as the asura agreed to give the dwarf three paces of land, the dwarf turned into a giant. In two steps, he claimed the earth, the atmosphere and the sky, which the asura had claimed as his dominion. He then looked at the asura and asked, 'Where should I place my third step? There is nothing left, because I have covered all the three worlds.'

At that moment, the asura realized the power of divinity. He may have conquered the three worlds, but divinity was

Vishnu as Trivikrama

greater than the three worlds put together. He also realized that he did not have the power to grant everyone's wish, as human hunger can rise infinitely like the giant, and the world's resources are always limited. He became aware of his hubris, and understood that this was Vishnu's attempt to remind him of his limitations. The asura bowed his head and said, 'With your third step, please crush my ego.'

Thus, the god, who in two strides had conquered the three worlds, placed his foot on the asura's head and crushed his ego. This pose of Trivikrama, one who has conquered the three worlds, is often depicted in art, with one foot on earth, the second foot on the asura's head, and the third foot stretching to the heavens.

The idea of three worlds is found in Hindu, Buddhist and Jain mythologies. In the Vedas, it described as the sky, the earth and the atmosphere. In the Puranas, it is described as the celestial realm of devas, the earthly realm of humans and the subterranean realm of asuras. With the influence of Zoroastrianism from Persia and later Christianity and Islam, we find the ideas of paradise, earth and hell entering Hindu and Buddhist mythology. Metaphorically, three worlds refer to the flesh, the psychological world within and the social world outside.

Just as Vishnu conquers the three worlds from the asura Bali, Shiva destroys the three flying citadels of the asuras known as Tripura, which is why he is called Tirpurantaka. Paralleling Vishnu's three strides are Shiva's three eyes and his trident, the Trishula. Shiva destroys these three worlds to reveal the soul or atma, hence the three horizontal lines of ash on his forehead.

Shiva's trident

In Buddhist mythology, below the earth are fettered creatures like asuras and nagas, and below that are the hells. Above the earth are the realms of the gods, and above that are realms of various Buddhas. Desire takes us below, and dhamma takes us above. Below is suffering and above is tranquillity.

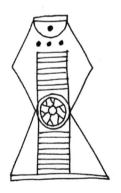

Three worlds of Jainism

In Jain mythology, the earth is the middle world, above the lower realm of serpents and below the realm of gods. Our karmic burden takes us to lower realms, and austerity removes our karmic burden and takes us to higher realms. Highest is the realm of the Jinas who have broken free from the wheel of rebirth.

This is the reclined (supta) variation of this asana, and it requires a lot of flexibility in the hamstrings and hip extensors. This could generally be considered a progression of Hanuman-asana (front splits) as it involves the same positioning of the legs. However, lacking the assistance of gravity acting on the torso to facilitate the stretch makes this asana more challenging. The final expression of this asana calls for standing upright and balancing on one foot.

57

Bhadra-asana
The Throne Pose

Ram is the only incarnation of Vishnu who is visualized as a king. As the eldest son of the king of Ayodhya, he was expected to sit on the throne, but on the eve of his coronation he was exiled to the forest for fourteen years. Ram obeyed without recrimination or regret. His younger brother, Bharat, whose mother's machinations had brought about this political calamity, refused to sit on the throne obtained so unfairly. Instead he placed Ram's sandals on the throne and ruled as regent until Ram's return. In Buddhist Jatakas, a similar tale is told but with a twist: Ram was told to leave for the forest by his father who feared his junior queen, Ram's stepmother, was plotting to kill Ram. The astrologers told the king that Ram would ascend to the throne only fourteen years later and so Ram is told to return after fourteen years. When the king died nine years later, Bharat begged Ram to return and be king.

But since Ram had promised his father to return only after fourteen years he refused to go back prematurely. Bharat then placed Ram's sandals on the throne and ruled as regent until Ram's return. In the Jain version of the Ramayana, Ram leaves for the forest to ensure that Bharat, who wants to be a monk, stays in the palace with his mother. All three stories focus on how Ram, though destined to be king, is

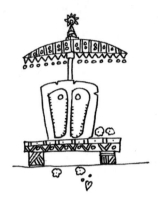

Ram's footwear on the throne

not attached to the throne. His brothers also show integrity by very publicly rejecting the ways of territorial beasts who fight over food and mates and for domination. That is why Ram is considered the epitome of dharma.

In Indic folklore, a king named Bhoja discovered the ancient throne of Vikramaditya buried in a field. Its base was made of the images of thirty-two yoginis. Every time Bhoja tried to sit on this throne, one of the yoginis would narrate a story about Vikramaditya, describing one of his traits that made him a legendary king. 'If you do not possess that quality and sit on this throne, we will drive you mad,' the yoginis warned. Bhoja cultivated each of the thirty-two traits and only then sat on

Vikramaditya's throne

the throne. Eventually he became as famous as Vikramaditya, ushering an era of peace, prosperity, generosity and justice.

The throne is an auspicious symbol that appears in dreams of women who will be mothers of Jain heroes, kings and sages.

Often referred to as Baddha Kona-asana (Bound Angle pose), this is one of the most powerful seated hip-opening poses in the practice. It can be a very good metric for determining when a practitioner is sufficiently prepared for more complex postures such as Padma-asana (Lotus pose) which require a lot of external rotation in the hips. Incorporating a forward bend into this position can greatly increase the intensity of the stretch through the inner thighs, and the reclined variation of this pose is often incorporated into many restorative practices. A key element to this asana is having the soles of the feet turned upward, and a good way to think of this is by opening the feet with the hands as if one was reading a book. When taking the forward bend in this position, it is important to remember that it is not necessarily about reaching the head towards the floor so much as it is about extending forward. Keeping the spine long and reaching forward with the chin can help achieve and maintain the necessary extension.

58

Setu Bandha-asana
The Bridge Lock Pose

In the fourteenth year of Ram's exile in the forest, his wife, Sita, was abducted by the demon-king Ravana, who took her to his island-kingdom of Lanka in the middle of the sea. Ram then raised an army of monkeys who built a bridge across the sea that connected the coast to Lanka. Ram and the monkey army crossed the bridge, defeated Ravana, rescued Sita and brought her home. This story is part of the great epic Ramayana, that speaks at length of kingship and the king's ability to rally the forces of nature, even when he is in exile, for a true king can raise resources even in the midst of the worst crises.

*Ram's bridge to Lanka
built by monkeys*

In the Thai version of the Ramayana (the epic travelled with sea merchants to South East Asia along with spices, gold and fabric), the Lanka end of the bridge built by monkeys was broken by Ravana. So Hanuman increased his size and stretched his tail so that Ram and his monkey army could walk on it to reach Lanka. Hanuman could do this awesome feat because he had yogic powers known as siddhi.

Mahakapi Jataka

This Thai story has strong links to the Mahakapi Jataka, where the Buddha-to-be was a monkey who helped his troop escape hunters by stretching between two distant trees and forming a bridge. The movement of the monkeys over his back broke his spine but he held on, helping them all escape.

The Mahabharata also speaks of a bridge of arrows shot by the great archer Arjuna. It connected earth with the sky so that Airavata, the mount of Indra, king of the gods, could descend from paradise during the elephant festival.

Arjuna's bridge to paradise

Arjuna then wondered why Ram did not build a bridge of arrows to Lanka to rescue Sita. The monkeys challenged him to build a bridge across the river that could bear the weight of a single monkey, let alone a monkey army. Sure enough Arjuna's bridge collapsed as soon as one monkey placed his paw on it. But then Krishna told Arjuna to chant the name of Ram and shoot the arrows. The bridge thus built was so strong that even when an entire troop of monkeys jumped on it, it stood firm. The monkeys and Arjuna realized, it was divine grace that created and stabilized the bridge, not merely strength or skill.

In the Puranas there are stories of two men meeting midway on a narrow bridge. Who gives the other right of way? The powerful or the wise? If the powerful gives way to the powerless it means he is wise and following dharma. However, the ego demands indulgence and like alpha beasts the powerful claim the right of way, which is adharma.

The concept of the bridge is very important in Jain mythology. The Jina is one who has conquered his passions. He is also called Tirthankara, one who found the bridge (or ford) that takes one out of the realm of rebirths. This bridge is made of Jain beliefs and practices.

Technically an inversion, as the heart is elevated above the head, this asana requires a great deal of stability in the core and strength in the neck. Most of the effort to lift into this asana is performed by the legs, but there are many modifications available to progressively work towards the full expression. Setu is the Sanskrit word for 'bridge' while bandha means to 'bind', 'lock', or 'tie together' (referring to the binding together or connecting of two land masses with a bridge).

59

Hanuman-asana
The Pose to Hanuman

Hanuman is one of the most popular gods in Hinduism. He is visualized as a monkey, but he is no ordinary monkey. He is a mighty monkey, extremely strong and very intelligent, and a great yogi. He is well-versed in the scriptures.

He is a poet, a musician, a magician, someone who can increase or decrease his height size, shapeshift and fly.

The sun was Hanuman's tutor. As a student, he stretched his legs from the eastern to the western horizon so that he could keep facing the sun's chariot all day and continue his lessons uninterrupted. As his tuition fee, he promised to

Hanuman

*Hanuman stretching
his legs across the horizon*

help the sun god's son Sugriva, who had been kicked out of his house by his half-brother, Vali.

Hanuman introduced Ram to Sugriva. The two made a pact: if Ram helped Sugriva become the king of monkeys, Sugriva, in exchange, would help him raise an army to defeat the demon-king Ravana. Hanuman then leapt across the sea to Lanka to locate Sita. In this incredible journey he had numerous adventures with various monsters. He helped Ram build a bridge across the sea so the army could go to Lanka, where they fought a war. During the war itself, when Ram's younger brother, Lakshman, was shot with a poisonous arrow, Hanuman travelled north and brought back a mountain of herbs to heal him. In art, he is often shown holding the mountain of herbs in his hand, crushing demons under his feet, his tail upraised, holding Ram's banner or his own mace in his hand.

Many consider Hanuman to be a form of Shiva and also the guardian of the Goddess. He is one of the few gods who is worshipped across all schools of Hinduism. He is much adored by ascetics, because he is celibate, in full sensory control, and believes in service for the other. He is a maha-siddha, one who possesses occult powers that allow him to change his shape and size, walk on water, fly through the skies and enchant any being. But this is tempered by his mystical union with Sita and Ram which is why he does not use this power to feel superior to anyone. He is said to live a simple life of contemplation in a banana forest, where he chants the name of Ram even today. In some temples, he is worshipped as Ramdas, the servant of Ram, seated at his lord's feet. In others he is worshipped independently as a five-headed being, with five pairs of hands, facing the south, scaring ghosts, demons and death itself.

In the Jatakas, the Buddha-to-be appears as Mahakapi, a great monkey who protects his troop of monkeys. He stretches himself between two trees so that they can easily run over his back and escape the hunters. He also tricks the crocodile whose mother wanted to eat his heart by stating that he had left his heart behind on his tree, forcing the crocodile to take him back to the riverbank.

According to the Kalpa-sutra, the fourth Jina of the twenty-four Tirthankaras of this eon, Abhinandan-nath, has a monkey as his symbol.

Jain Ramayanas, known as Padma-charitras, describe Hanuman as a vidyadhara, a celestial being with access to magical powers; not a monkey. He is considered one of the twenty-four Kamadevas born in every eon; Kama-deva is a man who is irresistible to women. He marries many women including Ravana's niece but eventually becomes a Jain monk.

Jina Abhinandan-nath

This posture loses a lot of its mythological potency when people call it the Monkey pose. Hanuman is not just any monkey, and the story of his leap across the sea to the island of Lanka is more than just a hop over a puddle. This was the greatest leap ever taken – across an entire ocean, when all hope was nearly lost, and the stakes were staggeringly high. Hanuman did the impossible, and this posture is a dedication to him and that greatest of deeds.

———————

60

Tola-asana
The Scales Pose

arada is a sage who loves to travel and to create trouble. One day, he came to Dwarka to meet Krishna. Krishna's eight queens welcomed him and offered to give him whatever he desired. The mischievous Narada said he wanted to take Krishna away. This request surprised the queens – how could they give their husband away! Anything but that, said the queens. So, the sage asked them to give him something equal in value to Krishna. The women wondered how they could find something that matched the value of Krishna. So, they had a giant scale brought to the

Krishna on a scale

courtyard and told Krishna to sit on one side of the scale, and placed something each of them valued most on the other side. Satyabhama offered her jewels, but Krishna seemed to weigh much more than all the jewels she had. Another tried to put all the fruit and vegetables she had, but that was not enough either. Finally, Rukmini, came with a sprig of the tulsi plant. She said it was the symbol of her devotion and placed it on the other side. Instantly, the pan lowered and Krishna rose high, indicating that her devotion to Krishna far outweighed Krishna himself. It was this sprig, the symbol of devotion, that she gave to Narada, who accepted it with grace.

Even today, in Krishna temples, a sprig of tulsi is used to remind us how the adoration of Krishna is far greater than Krishna himself. The problems of our life are not solved by Krishna, who is the mortal form of the immortal divine on earth, but by our devotion to him.

The idea of balance is of great value in Indic mythologies. In Hinduism, it is the balance of the material gaze of the householder and the spiritual gaze of the hermit. In Buddhism, it is the balance of wisdom and compassion that creates the Middle Path. This is very different from the way balance is seen as a symbol of fairness and justice in Western mythology: an eye for an eye, a tooth for a tooth. It is also different from the scales found in Egyptian mythology where the heart of the dead was weighed by the jackal-headed Anubis and the ibis-headed Thoth against the feather of Ma'at to see if the dead are worthy of making their journey to the afterlife kingdom of Osiris.

The earliest artistic representation of the tola (or tula) in the world, the equal arm balance, comes from Buddhist cave paintings of Ajanta in Western India, which are over 2000 years old.

In Buddhist and Hindu mythology, we learn of a king called Shibi offering shelter to a dove being chased by a hawk. The hawk then demands that the king feed him. The king offers him the meat of other birds but the hawk refuses saying why should the other birds die because this dove has royal protection. The king offers him the meat of animals but the hawk refuses, saying why should animals die because this dove has royal protection. Finally the king offers his own flesh, equal to the weight of the dove. The dove is placed on one pan of the scale and the king puts his flesh on the other. But the dove turns out to be so heavy that the king has to cut out all the flesh on his

Shibi Jataka

body. But the king persists, impressing the hawk, who turns out to be a god, wanting to test the king's commitment to dharma (in the Hindu retelling) and his compassion (in the Buddhist retelling).

The shape of this posture depicts a balanced set of scales where the plates float effortlessly in the air. I usually tell practitioners this posture is 'harder than it looks' – but not because it requires some inhuman amount of core strength. The problems most people face when attempting this posture are usually not related to strength or flexibility, but rather employment of improper technique. Think of it this way; if you're sitting on the floor with your spine straight, your shoulder girdle is as far from the ground as it can be (which is usually when someone says, 'my arms are too short'), but if you round your spine down a bit, *then* straighten your arms, you'll find significantly more ground clearance than when attempting this posture with a straight spine. In other words, the closer your shoulders are to the ground when your arms are bent, the higher you will be able to lift when you straighten them.

61

Hala-asana
The Plough Pose

In the Ramayana, when King Janaka of Mithila was ploughing the sacred field of the Goddess with a golden hoe, he found a child in the furrow. Janaka adopted this child and called her Sita. She became Ram's wife and accompanied him when he was exiled to the forest.

In the Harivamsa, which describes the childhood of Krishna, the plough is associated with Balaram. He uses it not only to plough fields but to divert the course of the river Yamuna, a mythic metaphor for canal irrigation. In Hindu mythology, when Vishnu takes the form of the cowherd Krishna, the serpent Ananta takes the form of Balaram, Krishna's elder brother,

Sita

who is a farmer. The two deities, Krishna and Balaram, embody the primary human occupations of animal husbandry and farming. In Jain mythology, Krishna and Balaram fight their enemy, Jarasandha, who attacks and burns down their city, forcing them to migrate from Mathura to Dwarka.

The island of Dwarka was ruled by a giant, who offered it to Krishna and his brother if one of them married his daughter, Revati, who was a giant as well. Revati's father had wanted the best groom for his daughter, so he had gone to the abode of Brahma in search of the ideal groom, not realizing that one day in the abode of Brahma is equal to 1000 years on earth. When he returned to earth with his daughter, centuries had passed, his kingdom had perished, and the world had changed so dramatically that the men and women were much shorter than in his time. His 'giant' daughter now could not find a husband. In order to see her face better, Balaram hooked his plough on her shoulder and tried to force her to bend down. But the moment he touched the plough on her shoulder,

Balaram

she shrank, miraculously, to his size. Thus, they were able to marry and Dwarka became the refuge of Krishna and Balaram.

There are stories in the Mahabharata where Balaram, angry with Kauravas, used his plough to drag their city of Hastinapur towards the sea, frightening all with his might.

In many schools of thoughts, Balaram is said to be a form of Shiva, for like Shiva, he loves to drink the narcotic hemp, is quick to temper, easy to pacify and very straightforward. This makes him very different from his charming, beguiling younger brother, Krishna.

Buddhist chronicles inform us that before he became the Buddha, Siddhartha Gautama of the Sakya clan watched his father participate in a ploughing festival. He noticed that while his father looked happy, the bullocks were not. He realized how our happiness blinds us to the unhappiness of others. Another time, when he asked a farmer for food, the farmer snarled, 'I plough, sow, reap and eat. What do you do?' To this the Buddha said that, he too ploughed, sowed, reaped and ate. He ploughed the mind with dhamma, sowed discipline, reaped mindfulness and ate the end of suffering. He shared his food with all, just as the farmer should.

Taking the shape of a field plough, this inversion requires a considerable amount of spinal flexion and shoulder mobility. It is essentially a progression from the position of Sarvanga-asana (shoulder stand – literally an 'all limbs' pose) where the feet are brought to the floor and the toes are pointed (representing the plough's blade). In addition to stretching the muscles of the back and shoulders, this posture can also offer benefits in terms of digestive health as the inverted forward-fold position gives the lower abdominal organs a gentle squeeze. Practitioners should be careful about the neck and the position of the head during such poses, and never turn their head from side-to-side when the neck is bearing additional load.

———

62

Bhuja Pida-asana
The Shoulder Pressure Pose

In the Mahabharata, Bhima was the strongest of the five Pandava brothers. He was so strong that when they were forced to seek refuge in the forest and save themselves from the murderous Kauravas, he carried all four of his brothers and their mother on his arms.

The Ramayana tells the story of Shravan Kumar, who carried a bamboo pole on his shoulder, from either end of which hung two baskets in which sat his aged father and mother. A similar tale is found in the Buddhist Jatakas, where the Bodhisattva is born as Jama who also carries his blind parents in baskets hanging from a bamboo

Bhima carrying his brothers

Kavad

sling. In the tale from the Ramayana, Shravan is killed by Dasharath, king of Ayodhya, a crime for which Shravan's parents curse him that he too will suffer separation from his beloved son, Ram. But in the Buddhist tale from the Jatakas, Piliyakka, king of Varanasi, who strikes Jama with an arrow, is forgiven by Jama's parents, as a result of which Jama is resurrected and their eyesight restored. The Hindu tale speaks of consequences of actions and the Buddhist tale speaks of the power of forgiveness.

This bamboo pole with weights on either side is called a 'kavad' and is a metaphor for worldly responsibilities that one is obliged to fulfil before one can be liberated from worldly life and the cycle of rebirth. It is also associated with Hidimba, Bhima's rakshasa brother-in-law. The story goes that when the sage Agastya was travelling from north to south India, he wanted to remind himself of the northern Himalayas. Therefore, he asked Hidimba to carry the mountain peaks on two ends of a bamboo slung on his shoulder. That is why mountains of peninsular India are said to be related to the northern Himalayas.

In the north of India, during the summer months many young men visit rivers and carry back water pots using the kavad. The pots must never be kept on the ground till they reach the local Shiva temple. A similar practice is seen in southern India, only here the kavad is symbolic, decorated with peacock feathers, reminding all of Hidimba's journey south with the Himalayan mountains on his shoulder sling. These mountains gave great pleasure not only to Agastya but also to Shiva's son Murugan, who preferred to stay in the south, away from his father.

The weight of the legs is applying pressure (pida) on the upper arms (bhuja) in this arm-balance posture. Balance in this asana comes from shifting the shoulders forward of the wrists to keep the body's centre of gravity (the hips) over the base of support (the hands). Gentle pressure is maintained in the fingertips to prevent falling forward, and keeping the head lifted with the gaze forward (instead of down towards the floor) is the ideal technique for finding and keeping the balance in this pose. When practitioners are first exploring this posture, it is usually approached from a standing position.

The legs are brought slightly wider than hip-width and a deep forward-fold position is assumed with the torso. Gradually, the shoulders work behind the bending knees as the hips begin to squat down. As the hips come lower to the ground, the upper torso must begin to lift (head up, gaze forward), otherwise the balance quickly becomes unmanageable. Once the feet come up, hooking one ankle over the other actually helps to consolidate the weight of the legs and bring them closer to the practitioner's centre of mass. This, in turn, allows the balance to be maintained without as much effort.

———————

63

Vatayana-asana
The Horse Pose

The sun took the form of a stallion to mate with his estranged wife, Saranya, who took the form of a mare. From this union were born the Ashwini twins, horse-headed gods who wanted to learn the secret lore of soma. However, Indra refused to teach them and said that the head of anyone who revealed the secret to them would burst into a thousand pieces. Finally, the sage Dadhich agreed to share the lore if the Ashwini twins could come up with a plan to bypass Indra's curse. The twins used their knowledge of medicine and surgery to replace the sage's head with that of a horse. Once Dadhich had revealed the secret lore using the

Surya and Saranya

Hayagriva

horse's head, it burst into a thousand pieces. The Ashwinis then reattached the human head to the sage's body. Since then, the horse is seen as the transmitter of wisdom. The Ashwini twins are equated with the Greek Discouri, twin horsemen of the skies.

In the Upanishads, it is the sage Yagnavalkya, who approached the sun to acquire knowledge. The sun took the form of a horse to give him the wisdom of the world. In the Puranas, Vishnu is sometimes visualized as the horse-headed one, known as Hayagriva. In this form, he rescues the Vedas and shares their wisdom with humanity.

When Vishnu wakes up and the world comes into being, he takes the form of a fish to reveal the secret of dharma and to establish culture, where the mighty take care of the meek. When it is time to end the world, Vishnu takes the

Kalki

form of the warrior Kalki, who rides a horse and, with his sword, destroys the whole world where everyone has abandoned dharma, choosing to live as animals in the jungle, where the mighty feed on the meek. This is Vishnu's violent form. Some people have equated this form of

Yoga Mythology: 64 Asanas and their Stories

Vishnu with the Four Horsemen of the Apocalypse found in Christian mythology.

In Buddhist mythology, the Buddha is closely associated with the horse Kanthaka, given to him when he was a prince. Riding this horse, he won many duels and competitions. While on a chariot pulled by this horse, he saw a diseased man, an old man, a dead man and a hermit – four sights that motivated him to seek the answer to life's sufferings. And finally, riding this horse he left

Horse chariot

his palace and escaped to the forest where he attained the heightened state of awareness known as Buddha-hood.

In Jain mythology, the horse is the symbol of the third Jina of this eon, Sambhav-nath.

Across India, we find terracotta horses being offered to village guardians who are visualized as carrying a sword and a spear in hand, riding a white horse, accompanied by a dog, and sometimes with a consort by their side. For centuries, various horsemen such as Greeks, Persians, Scythians, Parthians, Mongols and Turks entered India from the north-west, which linked the horse very closely to the martial tradition.

Jina Sambhav-nath

Similar to Garuda-asana but considerably more challenging, this posture steps it up a notch by incorporating one leg into a Padma-asana position and then coming down to a kneeling stance. Finding stability and balance in this position requires a lot of patience and practice, in the same way that finding stability and balance while riding a horse requires a great deal of patience and practice. As with any position that requires a half or full lotus, pressure on the knee joint can be considerable and proficiency in asanas such as Baddha Kona-asana (Bound Angle pose with a forward fold) is highly recommended. The binding of the arms is generally done after the kneeling balance is found and completely stable, but the posture can be modified by bringing the hands to the hips or extended out to the sides until the kneeling balance is sustainable.

64

Pinda-asana
The Ball Pose

Vishnu once took the form of a damsel called Mohini, or the enchantress. She appeared before the gods and demons in the form of a woman, tossing a ball (pinda) from one hand to the other. This made her look extremely alluring and beautiful. Both the devas and the asuras were so smitten by her that they were willing to do whatever she desired, to make her happy. She expressed the desire to distribute the nectar of immortality between them, and when they agreed, proceeded to pour all the nectar of immortality down the throats of the devas, without bestowing even a single drop to the asuras. The asuras realized this too late, because they were too beguiled by Mohini's beauty.

In the story, it seems that Vishnu, in the form of Mohini, is siding with the devas and opposing the asuras. This makes many people assume that the devas are the forces of good and the asuras are the forces of evil, but that is an incorrect reading of the story. Remember, there is no concept of evil in Hinduism. Vishnu bestows fortune on one group of people and leaves the other half hungry. This creates tension between those who have food and those who are hungry. This tension can only be resolved

Mohini

when those who have food share their food with the hungry. But the ones with food will never share it, because they feel they are entitled to it, as it was given to them by divinity and is a product of their labour. If the devas do not realize they should share food, they must fight with the asuras when the latter attack. Thus, the never-ending battle between the devas and the asuras, created by the enchantress Mohini, who loves to play with the ball, which bounces up and down like the alternating fortune and misfortunes of the gods and demons, continues in Hindu mythology.

Shiva Pinda

Pinda can also mean a stub or a lump. The Shiva-linga is often called Shiva-pinda by locals. In many stories, sages create the Shiva-pinda by piling sand on a beach, or by shoving an oval stone from a river bed into the sand of the riverbank. In the West, Shiva-linga is often translated as Shiva's erect penis, offending many Hindus who do not think of the Shiva-linga in such a way. For Hindus, the Shiva-pinda embodies the form of the formless. By not being carved into any particular form, the pinda indicates the primal 'unknotted' state of being. It represents the primordial pillar of fiery consciousness with no beginning or end that is being 'cooled' by water and contained in a trough, the water and the trough being symbols of the Goddess; she makes the transcendent immanent. Words like phallus and womb, stripped of symbolic meaning, and taken out of context, often trivialize complex metaphysical ideas and offer pedestrian titillation.

Pinda is also used for the ball or lump of mashed rice that plays a key role in the funeral rituals (shraadh) of Hindus. It personifies the bodies of the dead ancestors (pitr) as well as food for the deceased. Our flesh (anna-kosha) is made of food (anna) hence balls of mashed rice are used for the 'eater' as well as the 'eaten'. Eventually this pinda is given to crows who represent the dead in the land of the living (bhu-loka). Our ancestors are trapped in the

Offering to ancestors, pitr

land of the dead (pitr-loka) and yearn for a body so that they can experience life once more. Unless they acquire a body, they cannot practice yoga and so cannot break free from the wheel of rebirth.

Not just a clever name, the shape of the body in Pinda-asana looks very much like a ball. From the position of Sarvanga-asana and while balancing on the shoulders, one places the legs into Padma-asana and folds at the midsection to bring the knees down around the ears. Despite the compressed look, this posture is actually quite comfortable and relaxed, but it can take a considerable amount of practice to achieve the binding of the hands around the legs. As always, matters of personal safety cannot be overstated, and practitioners are reminded that the head should never be turned from side to side in positions like this. Additionally, it is strongly recommended to practice inherently risky postures (such as inversions and arm balances) under the guidance and presence of a qualified teacher (which no book or video recording can offer). Patient yogis and yoginis find health and happiness, but ambitious practitioners tend to get injured.

Conclusion
Metaphors of the Yogini

A yogi is typically visualized as being still, either seated or standing, while the yogini is constantly in motion – stretching, dancing, running, singing, flying. Taken literally, the yogi is the male practitioner of yoga who focuses on Vedanta mysticism, which leads to union with God, while the yogini is the female practitioner who focuses on Tantric occultism, that enables one to become God-like. Metaphorically, however, the meanings are quite different.

Yogi-Yogini

Yogi is who we are and can be (hungry, frightened, indifferent, empathetic, wise). Yogi is the dependent Brahma who can be the independent Shiva or the dependable Vishnu. Yogini is what we seek, want and have (food, beauty, wealth, power, knowledge). Yogini is Devi, wild (Kali) and domestic (Gauri), manifesting as resources (Lakshmi), power (Durga), knowledge (Saraswati), transformed by the yogi's gaze into either strength (shakti) or enchantment (maya). The two are gender-neutral concepts, complementing each other.

Like words, characters and plots in mythology are vessels (patra, in Sanskrit) to merely communicate ideas. They are symbols, not signs, meaning they have not one but multiple meanings. Their meanings shift as our sensitivity and awareness increase. The more we study, the more we share, the more we listen, the more our brain expands with understanding, experience and empathy, the more meanings and connections we discover.

Understanding is one thing but communication another. When the Buddha awakens, he realizes that speech reduces the depth of his experience, yet not communicating is not an option. When the Jina attains omniscience, he chooses telepathy to articulate that which defies articulation. Mythology uses a whole set of metaphors: from elements, plants, animals, artefacts, stories, geometry to astronomy. The enterprise can be frustrating but only if one assumes there is only one objective truth out there, rather than multiple subjective truths, constantly exchanging and expanding towards infinity.

The reason why access to ancient lore at one time demanded initiation was so that the teacher could guide the student gently into to the complex maze of metaphors. Metaphors were the mysteries. Mythology created the map to explore the unknown.

Sadly, the arrogance of modernity has led us to believe that people who lived before us were primitive, hence incapable of using metaphors. We assume those with lesser technology must have had limited access to human psychology. We find it hard to accept that the yogi and the yogini could be shorthand for concepts that defy language.

Flying yogini

In Jain mythology, the journey to the realm of Siddhas involves a journey through the realm of heroes (Vasudeva) and leaders (Chakravarti) before entry into the world of sages (Jina). The hero has a one-dimensional view of the world, the focus of an archer who sees only the target. The leader has a two-dimensional view of the world, like the perspective of a charioteer, who pays attention not just to his path but to also what is in front, behind and on the sides. The saint rises from the bottom and finally sits on top of the hill and so has a three-dimensional transcendental view, like a mountain-climber who realizes how tiny his village looks from above.

This viewer, the yogi, is the resident (dehi) of the body (deha). The Upanishads refer to the viewer as jiva or atma. Yoga helps

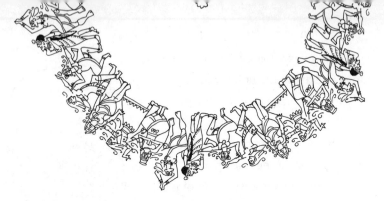

Circle of yoginis in a Tantric temple

us expand our gaze from one to two to three dimensions, to become more and more aware of our body, breath, emotions, thoughts, imagination, to our relationships with those around us, family, friends, strangers, plants, animals, elements, even ancestors. We notice the connections and disconnections like an archer, a charioteer, a mountain-climber.

Yoginis are the food for the hungry, the power for the frightened and the knowledge of the ignorant. They are what we seek. They are all things uncontrollable that we want to control. They are all things free that we want to possess. They form a ring around us. Facing inwards in Tantric temples that have no roof and facing outwards in Vedantic temples that enclose a deity in a closed chamber whose arches and

Circle of yoginis in Vedantic temples

pyramidal roof constantly remind us of mountain tops and the third-dimensional gaze.

The yogi looks within; hence shuts his eye. The yogini makes him open his eyes, look at the sky. Unless the yogi opens his eyes eventually, and flies with the yogini through the sky to mountain tops and into many different bodies and realms, vision will be limited, anchored, not free.

The tension between the yogi and yogini in yoga mythology is the tension between who we are or can be, and what we have or can have. Some yogis fear the yogini and seek to control her. Others reject her. Still others dance with her. These are metaphors for the human relationship with property – all that we claim as 'ours'. Do our possessions entrap us? Do they make us feel safe? Do they make us feel superior? Or do they liberate us? Just look at the rich around you; are they at peace? Or the powerful; are they tranquil? Or the beautiful; are they joyful? And the educated; are they wise? And those in love; are they less anxious than before? Or does wealth and power and beauty and knowledge and relationships make people as pompous as its absence makes people angry, frustrated and miserable. So many yogis who set out to liberate themselves from the world, end up creating hermitages where they become the focus of attention and the centre of attraction, trapped by the chuckling yoginis.

The thirty-two yoginis on Vikramaditya's throne remind Bhoja of the perils of wealth and power and knowledge. When Gorakh-nath draws his master Matsyendra-nath out of the banana forest, he is revealing the entrapping powers of the yogini. This is the reason why the Buddhas and the Jinas choose the hermit's way over the householder's.

But this is not rejection. They have simply let them go. They do not cling or shun, which is why they attract. They do not fetter, which is why they become magnetic. The yoginis who run away from those who seek to control them, return voluntarily when liberated.

Yoginis of Vikramaditya's throne

But when yoginis come voluntarily, can the state of tranquillity be maintained, or is it gradually eroded? Must the yogi keep his eyes firmly shut always, or risk opening them. In a never-ending world, the struggle has no eternal climax.

Darshan, gaze

In temples around India, the deity has large unblinking eyes. Above them are arches with heads of beings with large protruding eyes. And still above, atop the roof, are more heads staring at the people below. All these heads draws attention to our gaze (darshan). Our eyes can succumb to the enchantment of the alluring yogini. So the hermit shuts his eyes, and opens his third eye, burns desire, and rejects the yogini.

And yet images of yoginis are found in the very same temple – on the walls, forming a circle, facing either inside or outside. Some look like ordinary folk, two-armed. Others are extraordinary, with multiple arms, and heads and bodies of animals. Are they enthralling us with promises of power and knowledge, indulging our sense of self? Or are they giving us the wisdom to rise above our animal selves, overpower jungle law, and discover our divine potential – our humanity, our ability to care for others unconditionally? To understand, all we need to do is see images of Shiva and Shakti, Vishnu and Lakshmi, yaksha and yakshi, gazing lovingly into each other's eyes. The Goddess, or yogini, has shown them something we tend to ignore!

Our two eyes make us aware of, and dependent on, the material world. Our third eye helps us burn dependence and look beyond. The hermit seeks to shut two eyes and open the third eye in order to be independent. But the yogini encourages us to keep all three eyes open, so that we can be hermits who enjoy the household, and dance with the yogini as a yogi should, without feeling the need to control her. When all three eyes are open, we see who we really are, and the world as it really is, and become dependable.

Third eye

It is important not only to discover our divine potential (aham brahmasmi, I am divine) but also recognize the divine potential of that everyone around us (tat tvam asi, that's what you are too). When we recognize the infinite canvas of nature, in ourselves and in others, we realize the futility of control. Instead we are kinder to ourselves and others. We accept that others too can see like yogis, if they allow themselves to. We don't have to show them. For wisdom is all pervading, awaiting rediscovery, as it was in the infinite past, and will be in the infinite future. All we have to do, after discovering and enjoying and appreciating wealth, power, privilege and knowledge, is be generous enough to set the yoginis free so that they can fly into other people's lives.